HOW NOT TO GET SHOT BY THE POLICE

A Cop's Point of View

GERARD V. BEATTY

Note to readers of the Printed Copy:

For a full understanding of the issues presented in this book please go to my Web Site: gerardbeatty.com where you will find all of the web links in the electronic version listed by chapter to facilitate a greater understanding of police shootings and their aftermath.

You can click on those sites on your computer or iPad, etc. The web sites are very dramatic and necessary for the best reading experience.

Gerard V. Beatty

This book is dedicated to the men and women of Law Enforcement and to the New York City Police Department to which I owe so much.

Thank You.

Gerard V. Beatty

Web site: gerardbeatty.com

Library of Congress Cataloging-in-Publication Data

ISBN: 9781793815811

Web site: gerardbeatty.com

Library of Congress Cataloging-in-Publication Data

ISBN: 9781793815811

Table of Contents

Chapter 1: Moment of Decision:
The Factors that influence a Police Shooting . . 7

Chapter 2: Controversial Police Shootings 15

Chapter 3: Don't let the children fail.
If they do, they might find themselves
at the wrong end of a police firearm. 26

Chapter 4: Use of Force: Victims on both sides of the gun . 38

Chapter 5: Police Selection, Training and Reform
(A "Hotline" proposal) 43

Chapter 6: The Constitution and the
Use of Force – A Short Summary 51

Chapter 7: "Stop and Frisk": Taking guns off the street
and reducing the Homicide Rate 58

Chapter 8: Policing the Inner City 63

Chapter 9: Race, Politics and the Police 71

Chapter 10: It is not the color of your skin,
　　　　　your occupation or your Religion 86

Chapter 11: Lessons Learned – How not to get
　　　　　shot by the Police 94

Chapter 1

Moment of Decision: The Factors that influence a Police Shooting

A young police Sergeant and his driver park their marked car outside a Dry Cleaning shop on the West Side of Manhattan. The Sergeant has his uniform pants and jacket draped over his left shoulder and the driver grabs the door handle and opens the door for his boss. They look up in shocked disbelief as the clerk behind the counter has his hands raised and a black male with a gun is backing out of the store as they enter. Both officers pull their weapons as the man with the gun turns to face them with the gun a couple of feet away and pointed directly at the officers. The male suspect looks more surprised than the officers and time seems to stands still for precious seconds. The officers fire and hit the male at least six times. He does not fire and falls backward. He dies instantly.

This event happened in the 20th Precinct where I worked as a newly promoted Sergeant in the 1960's. It is not unusual and these events continue to happen.

All shootings are preceded by multiple factors that bring officers and perpetrators together in situations where they both must make instant decisions that often result in death and lasting pain for both sides in the shooting incident.

In that particular case, the deceased African American male was out of work and had a family with three children to support. It was shortly before Christmas. He was broke and like most people needed money to buy presents for the kids. He knew that the gun he carried was a fake and could do no harm. Desperate people are unpredictable. The highest rate for armed Robbery takes place in December for a reason.

The officers were blameless but were greatly affected after the facts became known. The Sergeant wanted to talk to the victim's family but knew that his thoughts or regrets might add to family suffering.

The shooting raised no concerns in the mostly white neighborhood. There were no protest marches and no civil or criminal action taken against the officers.

Never the less, the confluence of factors that lead to the shooting could have been changed so that the incident may not have occurred.

This book examines racism, protests, criminal justice and social reform and recent police shootings that have made the National news with a view toward creating conditions that would avoid these tragedies. I consider myself an expert on these kinds of events having experienced police shootings in every possible way. As a Lieutenant, I along with other officers produced the first or one of the first "Shoot, Don't Shoot" training films in the United States. It was titled "Moment of Decision". We duplicated several real shooting events that happened in New York City and used those to train officers before they were assigned to patrol. One of the proposals I make in the Chapter on Police Training is to use some of the recent controversial shootings to illustrate possible alternative actions that might prevent some but not all of these tragedies.

https://www.linkedin.com/in/gerard-beatty-25069136

As a Captain, I had to investigate many officer involved shootings and other events that the Department labeled as "Unusual Occurrences" in the South Bronx.

Disciplinary action or a recommendation of prosecution or re-training might take place in a police involved shooting incident. My friend Joe McNamara and I wrote or revised all of the disciplinary procedures for the NYPD. He became the Chief of Police of both Kansas City and San Jose, California. He was at our house for dinner with his wonderful wife shortly before his untimely death last year.

A brief analysis of recent shootings

The entire nation is aware of the turmoil that has been triggered by many recent shootings but often remain unaware of some factors that may have preceded or followed the shootings. We shall examine many of these events but from a different point of view with the goal of prevention. These are emotional events that open up the wounds of racism exacerbated by the media. They also feed the national frenzy and biases of both the left and the right.

Preceding Events

Every event has many causes. The Media reports some of the facts that come before a shooting but often mentions them in passing and concentrates instead on the sensational and the emotional reaction of the protestors and activists in the aftermath of the event. In most cases, we are unaware of what happened before the shooting that has a direct bearing on the cause the incident. We can never fully know what is on the mind of the actors involved but may construe some factors by the previous history of the people involved.

Attitude toward the Police

A person's attitude has a very large bearing on the outcome of any encounter between a citizen and the police. Many minority citizens have an attitude driven by a mistrust of authority and an expectation that the police will not treat them fairly. That kind of attitude makes people act defensively and they will be more likely to not cooperate with the officer's direction. The police have a great deal of discretion when it comes to the legal action they will take under any given circumstance.

A respectful, cooperative person is less likely to receive a ticket or even be arrested in minor instances. The law of arrest says that an officer "MAY" arrest for an offense based on Probable Cause, etc. The law does not say "MUST" arrest. This one word provides the officer with the ability to not arrest or not cite in many instances. If the offender gives the officer a hard time or mouths off, he will more likely be arrested or cited. It is human nature to give a person some respect and leeway, if that person is cooperative and respectful toward the officer. Justice is supposed to be blind but justice like beauty is often in the eyes of the beholder. A study by Albert J. Reiss illustrated this point statistically indicating that people are less likely to receive a citation or be arrested if they are respectful to the officer.

The Police and the Public, New Haven, CT: Yale University Press, 1971, pg 19.

Police Attitudes and conditioning

Having grown up in the heart of New York City has given me an advantage as a police officer. People that grow up in a "Lilly White" place in the suburbs and then become police officers may not understand the culture of the inner city. They may arrive on the job fearful of the public that they serve. Many shootings occur out of fear on the part of people on both sides of a firearm. It can be a "Culture Shock" if you don't know the area or the people.

Officers who have respect for people of all races and ethnicities are more relaxed and patient than officers who may have an authoritarian attitude and take instant offense at the slightest insult or failure to immediately comply with his or her direction. An officer must learn to restrain his impulses and his or her prejudices to prevent an outcome that may affect or end a person's life.

Drugs

Many of the victims of shootings involving the police were found to be under the influence of alcohol or drugs. This is not at all unusual in Homicide cases. In homicides committed by juveniles, it has been found that almost 70 % of the cases involved alcohol. In many cases it may be a combination of alcohol and drugs including PCP, cocaine, methamphetamine or marihuana.

Education and Jobs

The lacks of education or dropping out of school puts people at greater risk all of their lives. This factor affects their attitude; their ability to find work; to support their family and is highly correlated with the chances of going to prison. The police become the convenient scapegoats for all the ills of society and they have little control over the events they encounter in the Inner City that cause them to use force in an arrest situation. If you show respect and patience for everyone, you are less likely to get involved in use of force events. It is not easy. I would rather be involved in a clean "shootout" than deal with some of the drunks and addicts I have encountered. People under the influence of alcohol and drugs are very unpredictable, unreasonable and unmanageable. Restraint and patience are the hallmarks of a good officer but these qualities are hard to test for in police examinations.

Nature of the Offense and Police Response

The nature of the offense often dictates an officer's action. If you're responding to a felony in progress or a "Shots Fired", or a 10-13, "Assist Patrolman" the adrenaline rush can cause an overreaction to an event. Cops can become too excited and that can result in a serious but unintended mistake that could lead to an injury or death.

In some cases, making haste slowly is a good idea. An old time African American partner of mine gave me that advice when we were called to a knife fight down the street from where we were. Rather than run to the scene and be out of breath and get in between two people with knifes, it is better that the crowd inform the combatants that "the Police are here" so that by the time we get there the combat is over and all we have to do is arrest the combatants and take people to the hospital, if that is required. There are lots of street rules a cop can't learn in the Police Academy that can save his life. "Making haste slowly" to let people know the police are responding or already on the scene is sometimes a good idea unless a person's life is in danger and then any delay could be fatal.

Challenging people with weapons in their hands is often problematic. Always wearing a police vest and getting behind cover at the scene give you more time and options. Waiting for backup to arrive unless it is an active shooter situation should also be considered. If it is an active shooter situation, immediate response is the rule regardless of the danger to the officers. A quick response can save many lives.

The Aftermath of a Police Incident – The Greater Tragedy

People often forget in the drama of the moment that the aftermath of a police incident involving the use of force is often more tragic that the event itself.

The best illustration of this is the end result of the Rodney King riots. 54 people were murdered by the rioters following the beating of Rodney King. Everyone is aware of the Police brutality video and the beating of Mr. King but so few seem to know or care about these killings or the victims. We answer the question "Why" in the chapter on Race, Politics and the Police. The community and the media need to share the responsibility for these events.

Police Incidents are situational events between two or more human beings, many of whom have flaws. If an individual officer is biased or exhibits behavior that is not appropriate he or she should be removed from service and if the act is criminal, he or she should be arrested. The incident itself is not in any way reflective of all police officers or any law enforcement policy. The protests, more often than not, are generalized to all officers and generate animosity toward the police in general. Protests can be useful if they can right an individual injustice but in many cases they end up causing death and destruction.

A far worse and longer lasting effect is the destruction of trust between law enforcement in general and the public that is served by the individual departments.

One case on point was the protest march down Broadway in New York to protest the tragic case of Earl Garner which we analyze later in this chapter. This so called "peaceful" protest lead by some prominent African American politicians were chanting, "What do we want, Dead cops; when do we want it, Now".

https://nypost.com/2014/12/21/there-is-blood-on-hands-of-those-who-demanded-dead-cops/

The very next day two completely innocent human beings were shot in their patrol car by an African American gun man with a long criminal record. In many minds, the two events were related but no one took responsibility for encouraging the murderous act that followed the march and no apology ensued from the leadership that led the march. One of the black leaders marching with the chanters was a friend of both the Mayor and the President of the United States. Needless to say, most officers have a poor opinion of politicians who seem to condone such rhetoric by their silence on the matter. Sure, they condemned the shooting of the officers but not the rhetoric of the "Peaceful Protesters" who chanted the hateful words that may have led to the shooting.

One of the officers was of Asian descent and the other was Hispanic. They left behind devastated wives and children. Who was responsible and why were no arrests made for inciting people to murder police officers? Where was Justice this time? Mayor DeBlasio of New York a friend of the Al Sharpton who according to reports was involved in the protest march was tainted forever in the eyes of most officers in the department. They turned their backs on the mayor when he arrived at the funeral of both officers.

https://townhall.com/tipsheet/katiepavlich/2014/12/21/flashback-al-sharptons-marchers-in-new-york-city-chant-what-do-we-want-dead-cops-n1934308

Chapter 2

Controversial Police Shootings

The reader will find many dramatic police shootings that have been triggers for community protests and much violence scattered throughout the book. They are almost all related to race. White officers and Black suspects/victims cause the most community concern. If both the suspect and the officer are African American, a violent protest seems to be less likely. I can't recall any violent protests that were triggered by the shooting of a white suspect by a white or a black officer.

In mostly Caucasian communities, people may be upset by what they may consider an unjustified shooting but tend to wait for the investigation to reach a conclusion. White victim's families may sue the Police Officer and the related department but I can't recall a single violent protest over the shooting of a white suspect. Given that more white suspects are shot by the police than are black suspects, this seems extraordinary.

Trayvon Martin Case

Although the media and protesters like "the Black Lives matter group" always toss in the killing of Trayvon Martin in their list of police shootings of unarmed Black Americans, this was not a police officer shooting. The police did everything right when the dispatcher directed Mr. Zimmerman who was a "Neighborhood Watch" person to stop following Mr. Martin and wait for the police. He did neither. If he had followed police directions Trevon Martin would still be alive.

https://www.cnn.com/2012/05/18/justice/florida-teen-shooting-details/index.html

Eric Garner Case

Of all the cases I have analyzed, this is the most tragic case of all and should have been prevented. It is an egregious action by the Police on so many levels.

The offense was minor and caused by the lack of jobs and poverty in the Black Community. Mr. Garner was selling loose cigarettes on the street just trying to help support his family and being a good father. A store owner called the police. The police had no choice but to respond to the complaint.

The case reminded me that poor people who smoke may not have the money to even buy a full pack of cigarettes. That, in itself, is tragic. When I was a kid, maybe 12 years old, everyone smoked cigarettes including me. We used to go to the candy store near the corner put our pennies on the counter that was almost as tall as we were. Cigarettes were selling at about .20 Cents a pack and the store owner could make more money by selling loose cigarettes for a penny a piece. Things haven't changed that much for poor people. Poverty sucks!

No one wants to be arrested or hassled by the police for such a minor offense. Mr. Garner had been arrested over thirty times for similar minor offenses. On the video, he is seen resisted the officers. He was a very large man. It took a few officers to bring him to the ground but in doing so, they blocked his ability to breathe properly. I winced and became very angry when I viewed the video of the arrest. I was particularly upset by officer Pantaleo who had his knee on the man's neck. Mr. Garner was lying on his stomach with his neck stretched at a ninety degree angle to his body. He exclaimed that he could not breathe and by then, it was too late for anyone to help him. It was over in an instant as are most of these events.

The police officers involved had no idea that Mr. Garner had bad asthma and a weak heart. Had they known his condition, things might have been different. The officers did not break the law nor did they intend to harm Mr. Garner but I think his death could have been prevented with more patience and a little more talking. One of the officers, Patrolman *Daniel Pantaleo* was recently brought up on Department charges for using a choke hold which is against department policies. The punishment ranges from loss of pay to termination. Sometimes officers become impatient and that can lead to bad outcomes. I'm sure the officers involved have many regrets. Hindsight is still always 20 20.

Change in options

Patience must be a skill that every officer must have to prevent these kinds of events. Talking to people takes time. The officer must maintain a cool demeanor and take his or her time to resolve an event without using force. According to various studies, female officers have better communications skills than male officers. It is a hard skill to test for on entrance exams but it must be emphasized in the Academy.

Having Mr. Garner move away from the stores with a promise not to return may have worked. The officers have that discretion but perhaps Mr. Garner did not agree if he had already been arrested 31 times for similar offenses.

Perhaps the city should review these events and create a special space for street people to gather to try to make a living without breaking the law. It is and always will be difficult to find a good solution to poverty. This is a difficult video to watch.

https://www.cnn.com/2018/07/19/us/nypd-disciplinary-process-eric-garner/index.html

Michael Brown Case

Another tragedy related to drugs that led a young man to be shot by Police Officer George Wilson. Mr. Brown, 18 years old had just robbed a store of a pack of cigars which would probably be used, as was common, to stuff with drugs and smoked. The autopsy revealed the presence of drugs in this young man's system.

https://www.youtube.com/watch?v=mkOfqIXkBRE

The officer may or may not have known about the Robbery that was show on video tape from the store. It showed Mr. Brown pushing the small store clerk and menacing him when the store clerk confronted Mr. Brown and asked him to pay for the cigar pack which he was stealing. The definition of Robbery which is always a Felony dictates that if a person takes something of value by the use of force or fear, it is a Robbery.

According to the officer and Forensic evidence that backs up the officer, Mr. Brown shortly after leaving the store was walking with a friend in the middle of the roadway. The officer, in his patrol car, approached Mr. Brown and asked him to get out of the roadway. Mr. Brown did not comply and the officer started to get out of the car when Mr. Brown slammed shut the officer's door. The second time the officer attempted to leave the patrol car; Mr. Brown reached in, punched the officer and attempted to take the officer's gun. A shot was fired inside the car. Mr. Brown left the car and walked a distance away. The officer, with gun drawn attempted to arrest Mr. Brown, Mr. Brown rushed the officer with hands waving indicative of great annoyance. The officer, fearing for his life, fired and killed Mr. Brown. The body was left lying in the street for too long a time while waiting for the crime scene technicians and the coroner. This also angered the community.

https://www.youtube.com/watch?v=YVVmn14NnII

The Aftermath

Riots ensued in which out-of-control mobs burned down many businesses in the poor neighborhood including those owned by African Americans.

Two people were killed in the days that followed. One was a young man with a gun at the scene of a violent protest and the other one was a witness that testified in the Grand Jury hearing. He was found in a burned out car during the riots.

A few witnesses brought to the Grand Jury lied to investigators and under threat of arrest for perjury recanted their stories and admitted that they were not even present at the scene and wanted to try and help the family of Michael Brown in any subsequent civil action.

Three separate criminal investigations, one local, one state and one by the Federal Department of Justice ruled in favor of the officer and found that he had been justified in his deadly use of force. This did not end the violent protests and many people were arrested in the days following the shooting.

People upset by a police shooting must recognize that the legal system has mechanisms in place to thoroughly investigate these events but it takes time. Just as we expect officers to be patient, we also expect civilized people not to condone or join a mob of criminals that can destroy a community.

Often, the criminal element in a poor community seizes upon unrest to burn and loot stores. Some of the more sane leadership in these communities tries to foster peaceful protests against what may be seen as an injustice perpetrated by the police department and the entire Criminal Justice system. Peaceful protests are one thing but in many cases the leadership not only fails the community but fosters violence by their rhetoric. The rhetoric of hate and emotional chants such as "Hands up, don't shoot", which was an entirely false claim in the Michael Brown case, serve to further inflame the rioters. Celebrities or football players wearing socks or shirts that portray the police as "pigs" are not helpful or conducive to creating good community-police relationships.

The long term distrust of law enforcement may even be more destructive. In the emotional turmoil of the moment magnified by the media who seem to seek out the most biased voices in the community serve to further inflame the situation and destroy confidence in the Police. This was the case in the aftermath of this case as the reporter for CNN seemed to deliberately pick out the most anti-police activists to interview. Reporting should have concentrated instead on the random acts of crime, looting and destruction caused by the rioters. It is my opinion that the riots that follow some of these events would be far shorter if the media focused on the criminal acts of the rioters rather than the officer's actions. The officer, if he or she was acting illegally, will be held accountable by the courts and prosecutors.

The Alfred Okwera Olango Case

In the released video of this officer involved shooting, the victim, who was acting erratically, refused the officers direction to take his hands out of his pocket. As the Chief of Police reported and the video confirmed:

"El Cajon Police Chief Jeff Davis said at a news conference: "At one point the male rapidly drew an object from his front pants pocket, placed both hands together on it and extended it rapidly towards the officer taking what appeared to be a combat shooting stance, putting the object in the officer's face," El Cajon Police Chief Jeff Davis told reporters.

https://www.nbcnews.com/news/us-news/videos-released-officer-fatally-shooting-alfred-olango-el-cajon-california-n657746

In this particular case, the victim's sister indicated that her brother had mental problems. Whenever a person acts as though they are going to shoot the responding officer, the officer has no idea of the person's mental condition. He only thinks that he is about to be shot and killed. A sane person would not act in this manner unless they were completely distressed or depressed and in a suicidal mode of behavior. Some of these cases are well known as "Suicide by Cop".

https://ajp.psychiatryonline.org/doi/full/10.1176/appi.ajp-rj.2017.120107https://www.nbcnews.com/news/us-news/videos-released-officer-fatally-shooting-alfred-olango-el-cajon-california-n657746

A Noble Gesture or "Suicide by Cop"?

We may never know what is in the mind of a victim or officer in a police shooting but all we can do is speculate about the motives of both the officer and the victim.

In some of these cases, it can be "speculated" that the victim purposely put himself in jeopardy of being shot or injured by the police in a valiant attempt to help his family. We can have some empathy for a man who may have been a felon unable to obtain a decent job who feels guilty about his past life and not being able to help his kids or family. He will most likely be depressed and may be contemplating suicide. As a last gesture, he might conceivably put himself in jeopardy hoping that his kids and family might benefit from a wrongful death suit.

This is complete speculation on my part but some circumstances lead me to this possible motivation. It is well known in inner city communities that a legal action following what could be construed as an unjustified death or injury caused by police action can lead to large monetary settlements by the jurisdiction involved.

The Keith Lamont Scott Shooting

The videos taken at the scene of Mr. Scott's shooting along with the forensic evidence indicates that Mr. Scott had a gun in his hand at the time he was shot and killed by the police. His wife was at the scene at the time of the shooting and was filming the encounter with her cell phone. Mr. Scott is seen getting out of his car, allegedly with a gun in his hand, and his wife is clearly heard saying over and over, "Keith, don't do it", "Keith, Don't you do it" or "Don't you F_ _ _'en do it". It is evident that we do not know what was in the mind of Keith Scott but the wife refers to some action, she knows he may be thinking of taking. It seems plausible that Mr. Scott and his wife discussed the "IT" that she is yelling at him not to do?

https://www.nbcnews.com/news/us-news/no-charges-killing-keith-lamont-scott-whose-police-encounter-was-n690126

Could Mr. Keith Scott be committing suicide or is he sacrificing his life trying to help his family in a subsequent legal action if a Civil Court find that the police shot him without justification?

We may never know what "IT" means but clearly his wife has that answer. It is unclear from the angle of the videos taken by the police or Mrs. Scott whether or not Mr. Scott had a gun in his hand or if he has pointed the gun at any of the officers. We will have to wait for the results of any further investigation or court case to determine any further facts in this police shooting. We might be able to rule out police officer bias since the officer who shot Mr. Scott was also African American.

The wife of the victim filed a wrongful death lawsuit against the Police Department for the killing of Mr. Scott.

https://abcnews.go.com/US/family-files-lawsuit-fatal-2016-shooting-north-carolina/story?id=57497800

The Laquan McDonald Case

McDonald was a 17 year old boy walking in the middle of the street with knife in his hand, followed by a couple of officers with guns drawn directing the 17 year old to drop his knife when officer Jason Van Dyke arrived at the scene. The officers related at the trial that they were waiting for an officer equipped with a Taser weapon to arrive at the scene. Officer Van Dyke arrived and within a short time fired and hit the young man. The first shot knocked the boy down and from the film; it appears that the young man is no longer a threat to the officer. Officer Van Dyke kept on firing fifteen more times. This was clearly using excessive and unnecessary force. Van Dyke said that he felt his life was in danger but the video seemed to indicate that the boy was veering away from the officers.

The officer was subsequently arrested for first degree murder, aggravated assault and official misconduct. He was convicted at trial and is awaiting sentencing. Here is the dramatic video taken by a couple of dash cams on the police vehicles.

https://www.nytimes.com/interactive/2015/12/04/us/questions-in-laquan-mcdonald-shooting.html?action=click&module=inline&pgtype=Article&region=Footer

The officer was convicted of 2nd Degree Murder and 16 counts of aggravated assault. One count for each of the 16 bullets fired at the young black man.

https://abc7chicago.com/jason-van-dyke-trial-chicago-officer-found-guilty-of-2nd-degree-murder/4417237/

Terrence Crutcher Shooting

Mr. Crutcher, a 40 year old Black male was acting erratically and walking in the middle of a roadway where he stopped his vehicle. The police were called and attempted to stop him but he repeatedly ignore the officer's direction to stop and get down on the ground. He did at one point put his hands up in the air as he walked away from four officers who had guns or Taser weapons drawn. He reached his car and appeared to have both hand on the car but also appeared to be

reaching into the car when Officer Shelby fired her weapon and another officer simultaneously fired his Taser. Mr. Crutcher was found
to be under the influence of at least two drugs including PCP. As I
indicated elsewhere, the vast majority of these controversial shooting
involve drugs found in the suspect's system.

Be aware that this is also a dramatic video.

https://www.washingtonpost.com/video/national/dashcam-video-
shows-police-shooting-of-terence-crutcher/2016/09/19/8e7a5c0e-
7ea3-11e6-ad0e-ab0d12c779b1_video.html?utm_
term=.1d8b6f3e4d6c

Officer Shelby was subsequently arrested for murder and tried but
was acquitted of all charges. Here is a video of the trial and acquittal.

https://www.foxnews.com/us/terence-crutcher-case-oklahoma-
officer-betty-shelby-acquitted-in-deadly-shooting

Chapter 3

Don't let the children fail. If they do, they might find themselves at the wrong end of a police firearm.

A Personal Story

I was a street kid, born in Harlem, a good student with straight "A's". At the age of 12, I held two part-time jobs after school and was paying half the rent. I also had an illegal job on Saturdays delivering booze to the poor. However, with no support system at home and two alcoholic parents, I was forced by the system to drop out of school in order to pay all of the bills for my family.

We went to the welfare system to see if we could get just a little help when I turned 15 so I could stay in School. The African American case worker looked at the application, looked up from her desk and said to my mother, "You don't need welfare , you're White and you have a big white boy" I took my mother's hand and said, "let's get out of here; we don't need their help" I quit school the next day and got a full- time job washing and busing dishes at one of the many "Good Old Horn and Hardart Automats", a very popular fast food restaurant chain unique to New York City at the time. The job included meals and I made about $33.00 for 40 hours work. Those were the "Good Old Days".

Society has a responsibility to make certain that all children are safe, become educated and gain the rights to "life, Liberty and the Pursuit of happiness" that is the promise of the Constitution.

Far too often children fail because of a lack of support at home or in the school system. Some ignorant and affluent people who have been blessed with a support system say it is their own fault for not studying hard enough or staying in school. Easy for them to say!

Many children live in dysfunctional homes without a full family. The father may be absent or unknown, with a mother that works two or three jobs to pay the bills. These kids literally grow up in drug infested streets ruled by local gangs. I was one of these kids but my Washington Heights neighborhood was decent compared to most of the inner city neighbor hoods where I worked throughout my career. I know how easy it would be to fail.

How can we help these kids? Helping people succeed is what this book is all about. We cannot let our children fail nor can we keep putting millions of people into the criminal justice system because they did not get the help they needed so desperately when they were children.

Educate of Incarcerate

America is one of the wealthiest countries in the world but we would rather spend more money incarcerating people than educating our children. Right now, California is spending over $75 ,000. a year to keep a person in prison and spending about $10,000. to educate a child and keep them in school.

http://www.latimes.com/local/lanow/la-me-prison-costs-20170604-htmlstory.html

If we reverse those figures, we can reduce the prison population to a necessary minimum. If we don't spend our tax money on the front end which is education, we will surely have to spend it on the back end which is the prison system.

The truth is that we know what the problems are but lack the political will to do anything about them. I have several proposals to reform this totally insane school and correctional system.

Correlation between dropping out of High School and Imprisonment

We have known for decades that there is a very strong correlation between educational attainment and imprisonment. The higher your level of education, the lower is your chances of going to prison. Education is the key to success and we should never let our children fail.

A tragedy in the making

My stepson dropped out of High School despite my best efforts to keep him in school. He came to live with us at the age of 12.

I had raised my five children as a single parent for many years of their life and all of my children have been very successful including two that were either valedictorian or salutatorians in High School. I remarried and gained an enlightened wife and a stepson who was very bright and highly capable but he had a very low self–image.

It is my belief that my stepson would also have been very successful if teachers and administrators were more concerned about making sure all students stayed in school than worrying about the school's average Grade scores.

He was caught smoking pot and the school wanted to expel him for that and the fact that he was not doing well in school. I went so far as forcing a meeting between myself and the principle along with his teachers and a vice principle of the High School. The school has a wonderful academic record and seemed very anxious to let him leave as his marks were lowering the class average of which they were justly proud. I guess they had forgotten their responsibility to educate all of the children in the area including those that were having problems. He was present at the meeting and got the clear message from school administrators that he was not wanted. He finally expressed his mistaken desire to quit school despite my best efforts to keep him enrolled. I could do nothing. He died at the age of 22 years from a heroin overdose.

Keeping kids from failing

I became a High School drop out because of a total lack of support from my family or "the system". I managed to obtain a GED with a very high score which got me into John Jay College of Criminal Justice. My first career was in Law Enforcement and I retired as a Captain with the NYPD. It took me a while but Along the way at the age of 43, I earned a B.A., Magna Cum Laude and with the help of the NYPD, I obtained a couple of Graduate Degrees. More recently, I have been a Professor at three well-known Universities and a four year college.

In between and during my teaching career, I founded and ran a Private Security corporation employing about 140 people.

It has been a long and bumpy road but I still love the journey. But this book is not about me. It is about changing the system so that children have the support they need to succeed. It is also about reforming the Justice System to bring a measure of sanity and common sense to a sometimes broken system.

Proposal

Most High School drop outs start to need help in the first grade and if we don't act early enough, the child will fail. Kids who are not doing well and have no help at home, become discouraged by their lack of progress and eventually give up. When you have no hope, it starts a downhill spiral that ends in the prison system. Teachers know who needs help but do not have the proper resources to make up for the lack of family support. The school system does not have the funding to reverse educational failure for these at risk kids.

I propose in each public school system, creating a position called "Volunteer Coordinator" (VC). His or her responsibility will be to identify "at risk kids" and hook them up with individual tutors and student interns. I know that some progressive schools are doing some of the latter already. Good students' helping those falling behind is an excellent idea but It is not enough. We cannot hope to monitor the support of failing kids unless we create a position in each school that will be responsible for creating and directing a support system for the child. Later I will show how we can pay for this position by shifting funds from the correctional system and creating other funding sources.

The VC would recruit student interns who would earn school credits or other perks. The VC would find retiree and other volunteers for individual students to help them with homework and encourage them to study and complete assignments. Some volunteers, if qualified, could start after school clubs or after sports activities. There are literally thousands of retired and working people who would be more than willing to help. This could be done over the Internet or after school at the school library. To help these tutors, the volunteer coordinator would provide them with a list of various resources and readily available software that is excellent to aid in understanding various subjects and to provide children direct access to learning resources such as computers and software. The VC would communicate with the child's parents to enlist their support for this program. There is abundant learning software available to students and their tutors in each grade and some of these are free. An Internet resource such as the "Khan Academy" online is just one excellent and free example.

All tutors would have to be vetted by the local sheriff's or Police Department. Under no circumstances will an adult tutor be left alone with a young student except over the Internet and that can also be monitored easily by spot check monitoring by the person running the program.

Many capable and educated retirees are ready and able to help students in need and are looking for opportunities to find a purpose for their lives, My wife and I volunteer for many causes and this selfless service is one of the fastest paths to enlightenment and earthly satisfaction. Retirees find that helping others is extremely helpful and they gain more from it than the people they are helping.

Grant Writing Position

Another responsibility of the VC would be to raise funds and write grants to private foundations to support this proposal. Bill and Linda Gates, are you listening?

Paying for these Proposals: Shifting funds from the Prison systems to the Schools

Ideas are not worth the paper they are written on without a means to pay for them.

The Volunteer Coordinators position would be paid for in a State like California by the selection of just one or two non-violent inmates for release into the community under house arrest monitoring or placement in a residential facility. We would shift funds from the correctional system for each VC position created at every school in the state that is identified as a failing school in the inner city.

The Grant Writer

(GW) previously mentioned would obtain funds to pay for computers, software programs and Internet resources. Internet resources would include places like the "Khan Academy" and software to facilitate online communications between students and tutors. As a Professor, I have created many Internet Courses for multiple Universities and Colleges over the past 30 years and perhaps we can create special internet courses to help failing students at both the elementary and High School levels.

Charity begins at Home

I would also appeal to the cadre of very generous American Billionaires that have created charitable foundations to help these children. Many of these successful people had a good support system growing up and it is time to give back some of their blessings by helping and giving hope to thousands of kids in this country. Too many times, we see charitable foundation money going to overseas causes when we have so many problems at home. When we lift the poverty stricken bottom rung of our society we will create a more just society.

Jesus said, "Whatever you do for the least of me, you do for me"

The Head Start Program

The earlier a child begins to learn, the less likely he or she will fail when regular school begins. The Head Start Program has helped many children and funding for such programs should continue at an accelerated pace particularly for at risk families.

A Student's Responsibility

Of all the things, I have ever learned it is that **True Change comes from the inside out and cannot be imposed from the outside in.** That is one of the major flaws in our correctional system. When we try to change people through a system solely based on punishment. It does not work.

However, having said that, like it or not, not everybody has the same capacity for learning and we have an obligation to help those who have a deficient capacity for success including children without a support system. They are shaped by all of the social, psychological and biological influences that shape every one's life and we need to help them. However, we cannot completely abandon an individual's responsibility for the consequences of their own behavior.

I cannot emphasize enough that the individual student bears the main responsibility for his or her own learning. But it has to fall within the realm of their capability. Give people an equal opportunity and the rest is up to them.

The Carrot and the Stick Approach to Change (Behavior Modification)

Keeping in mind, an individual's growing responsibility to be the master of their own life, we can approach families and kids at risk with this in mind. Families and children at risk can be identified by their behavior. Incentives both positive, which is the better alternative, and negative can be devised to facilitate change.

The positive approach – The carrot

We have already proposed changes in the educational system to provide resources to help children succeed in school. The money can be raised through an ongoing transfer of monies away from corrections, and provided to schools to make sure children are provided with adequate nutrition at school and to make sure that the children are all attending school. Getting a personal Computer to use for school would certainly be a great gift for any student.

Negative consequences for bad behavior – The stick

If a child is truant from school or refuses to accept the help he or she needs to Graduate, there should be consequences for those decisions both for negligent parents and the child.

The Motor Vehicle Bureau rules could be amended to include that no license shall be issued to any child under the age of 18 years who has is not in school or has not finished High School. Exceptions to the law will include kids that are required to work because of family necessity but that must be verified.

State School attendance law shall be amended to include a section that includes but is not limited to Cell phones found in possession of a child under the age of 18 years who is absent from school may be legally confiscated by a teacher, truant officer or police officer and held by the police or school administrator until the student and his or her parents mutually agree to make sure that child is regularly attending classes. This idea sounds harsh but kids need structure and discipline to help them focus on staying in school. When they go back to school, they would get their cell phones back.

Kids love their cell phones and this punishment would certainly get their attention and may keep them in school!.

Juvenile Offenses

Any child under the age of 18 years who commits a juvenile offense that would have been classified as a felony is he or she was an adult and is therefore called an act of "Delinquency" and is incarcerated in a juvenile facility shall not be released from probation or from the facility until that student successfully complete a High School education. All juveniles and adults on Probation or Parole would be required, under the law, to complete their High School education or, at the least, a GED before being released.

Correctional reform Proposals

The purpose of this book is to prevent people from failing and finding themselves on the wrong side of a police firearm or in prison. I am advocating several proposals designed to keep people out of the Criminal Justice System. The savings from these programs will the transfer to the educational system. As I said before we either educate people and help them or incarcerate them when they fail.

I consider myself an expert on Police Shootings but I also have considerable experience in the field of corrections.

My wife and I have been to many state and federal facilities as part of a non-profit project team that teaches inmates how to meditate. I was also the keynote speaker for a graduating class of inmates at Soledad Prison in California. About 350 Inmates were graduating with certificates in plumbing, painting, auto repair, carpentry, guitar making, and other skill sets. Some had completely their High School GED diplomas. I had started the first Internship program in Criminal Justice at a community college and had students doing internships at the prison, half-way houses, the D.A.'s and Public Defender's offices along with the Sheriff's office and the local Police Departments.

At the present time, I am a county advisory chairperson for a non-profit corporation called "Turning Point". The organization helps both federal and state inmates, parolees, probationers and juveniles conform to the needs of society and stay out of prisons and other facilities. Board members include representatives of Parole, Probation, Sheriff's Department, employment division, restorative justice, mental health and other community groups.

Proposal: Sentencing offenders to school instead of prison

I wrote a grant proposal in 1998 to the Federal Office of Juvenile Justice and Delinquency Prevention. Its purpose was the diversion of at-risk juveniles to a community college as a sentencing option: a collaborative effort between the Criminal Justice and Educational systems. It could also be extended to adults who had committed non-violent crimes.

At risk people would be sentenced to a community college where they would have to meet certain educational goals rather than be sentenced to jail or prison. A probation officer and a college counselor would monitor each person sentenced under this proposal to help them succeed. I was a finalist for the large grant but the college administration did not support the proposal and it was not granted. It was my understanding that the administration was afraid of legal liability for having at- risk people assigned to the college by the court. It was short sighted in that if people fail they will surely become threats to the community. Perhaps the same proposal would now be acceptable. It would substantially reduce the money we now pay the prison system keep a person in prisons. When people are successful they also pay taxes which would be a further dividend.

Alternatives to Prison

Extending <u>Restorative Justice</u>, which is a program that aims at reconciliation between the offender, the community and the victims of crime. It keeps people out of the CJ system and does not stigmatize them with a criminal record of any kind. The program restores offenders back into the community.

    <u>House arrest</u> is one of the least expensive alternatives to incarceration and should be employed much more often. The offender is under either probation or parole supervision and is required to wear an electronic monitoring device. It costs an average of $6. per day as opposed to almost $100. per day in a local jail and $75,000 a year in some State Prisons.

Chapter 4

Use of Force: Victims on both sides of the gun

Statistics on the Use of Force

The use of force by the police is fairly rare when you consider some of the following studies and statistics.

The Federal Government has conducted research that estimated that approximately 144 Million contacts occur every year between civilians and the police; of these about 500,000 involve some use of force. These incidents are found to be:

> "unrelated to the officer's personal characteristics, such as age, gender and ethnicity. It is more likely to be situational—for example, when police are trying to make an arrest and the suspect is resisting. Force is more likely to be used

with special populations, such as people under the influence of alcohol or drugs or mentally ill individuals" (*Introduction to Criminal Justice, Joseph Senna and Larry Siegel, 9th Ed. Pg.244*)

Fatal Shootings by the Police

According to the Washington Post Data bank, it is remarkable and may be a bit shocking to most people that Police Officers have fatally shot almost 1000 people every year for the past four Years.

2015 = 995 people

2016 = 963 people

2017 = 987 people

2018 = 766 up to October 15th

This database is very interesting and discloses that in 2018 about 242 of these suspects/victims were Black or Hispanic and 292 were white. The statistics are extraordinary in that only 13 percent of the population is Black. Perhaps the statistics are a reflection of the violent crime rate among African Americans in general.

Most of the suspects either had a gun or knife. 24 suspects had a toy weapon and 35 were unarmed. Over the span of two years 86 people were killed who were showing toy guns that look very real but turned out to be fake. A fairly large number of people were determined or thought to be mentally ill but the exact number is unknown because of the privacy laws governing medical information (HIPPA laws). The information above was extracted from the following web site:

https://www.washingtonpost.com/graphics/2018/national/police-shootings-2018/?utm_term=.4c3b12eec6de

The Larger and More Important Hidden Problem that No one wants to Address

Black on Black crime is a far larger problem that the problem of the few controversial police shootings that occur each year but that problem is largely ignored by politicians and the liberal media.

In 2017, homicide rates by gun among African American males were ten times more than among white males. We had the highest rates of homicide by gun in 2017 than any other year the past 40 years. The homicide rate among blacks was 33 per 100,000 black males and the rate for white males was only 3.5 per 100,000. Almost every city that has arrested an officer for a controversial shooting or using too much force the past two years has experienced a large increase in violent crime.

https://www.cnn.com/2018/12/13/health/gun-deaths-highest-40-years-cdc/index.html

The seemingly constant criticism of Police Officers in the press has resulted in making many officers reluctant to confront anyone. This results in higher than normal homicide rates in high crime areas. Why should an officer confront a suspect, if he or she can just ignore dangerous situations and safely retire in 20 or 25 years?

We need officers to investigate and "Stop and Frisk" suspects to take guns and criminals off the streets. When they do a good job, they put themselves in jeopardy of being criticized, shot, fired or arrested! There was an old but still true saying among officers in the NYPD.

"The more work you do, the greater your chances of getting into trouble".

The Police as victims

I went to the funeral of several officers while I was with the NYPD. The number seems to be increasing over time.

"A total of 73 law enforcement officers have been killed in the line of duty during the first half of 2018 -- a 12 percent increase over last year." according to a preliminary report from the <u>National Law Enforcement Officers Memorial Fund</u>.

I believe as of this year's date, 44 were killed by assailants and 32 were killed in vehicular accidents.

As a young sergeant, I was aware that the families of fallen officers needed immediate assistance when their main support is killed in the Line of Duty. On my own, without Department knowledge or approval, I wrote a New York State Bill that automatically gave the family an infusion of money. At that time, I believe the sum was only about $25,000. I sent the Bill, after learning how to write legislation, to Representative Edward Speno who was a retired officer. I can't remember what Police department he was retired from. That sum of money, I believe has grown to $100,000 or more. He sent me a letter of appreciation and got the bill passed. He passed away long ago.

The average number of officers killed each year is 151.

In addition, 49.409 cops are assaulted and 13,424 receive Injuries as a result of those events.

<u>http://www.nleomf.org/facts/officer-fatalities-data/daifacts.html</u>

During 2017, 140 Officers committed suicide. It is a stressful occupation and most of us have some form of PSTS most of it undiagnosed. Officers are very reluctant to seek help or even talk about some events even to their families.

https://www.usatoday.com/story/news/2018/04/11/officers-firefighters-suicides-study/503735002/

The first traumatic event I experienced as a young officer, I related to my wife that night and she said that she did not want to hear about any more of my horrific experiences on the job. They were too upsetting for her which made it difficult for me as well.

Chapter 5

Police Selection, Training and Reform (A "Hotline" proposal)

Standards for Selection

The standards for the selection of police officers need to be very high. Picking the wrong officers can be a disaster in terms of the safety of the public. The power of arrest comes with it a deadly attachment and that is, the power to use deadly force when it becomes necessary.

Some departments such as the New York City Police Department have very high standards others have had to lower their standards in order to recruit enough officers.

I have been retired for a while and hope that the NYPD still maintains its high standards. When I came on the job, the Department had over 10,000 applicants. By the time, these people went through the background and the written test, the physical agility and medical exam; only 100 people were able to enter the Police Academy.

"It's estimated that more than 90 percent of law enforcement agencies in the United States require the psychological screening of their applicants. By comparison, only about 65 percent use a <u>polygraph exam</u>, and 88 percent employ drug screening."

https://www.thebalancecareers.com/psychological-exams-and-screening-for-police-officers-974785

In addition, it is recommended that the Police Force should closely resemble the population it serves. Some departments do a great job at recruiting minority groups. Again, the NYPD excels in this effort with about 52% of the entire force composed of minority officers. Another consideration is to recruit officers who have a good understanding of the cultural diversity of the area to which they will be assigned. Growing up in the city of New York gave me an advantage over white guys that came from the mostly white suburbs. You really need to know the cultural makeup of the area where you're going to be assigned or it can be a problem for you and the good citizens of those tough areas.

When I was about to be assigned as a Precinct Captain to a largely Hispanic precinct in the city, the department sent me to a Spanish language school for three full months to not only learn the language but the culture as well. It was well worth the time and money.

I was assigned to the highest crime precinct in Harlem when I graduated from the Police Academy. Throughout my entire career, when I worked the streets, I was almost always assigned to the busiest Precincts in the city including Harlem, the South Bronx, Bedford Stuyvesant and Brownsville in Brooklyn.

It is very difficult for a department to find officers with the right temperament for the job. To be patient, compassionate and be able to restrain oneself in the face of the most extreme forms of provocation can be very hard. An extensive background investigation is the best means of finding the right officers. Past behavior is the best indicator ow future behavior. Yes, people can change but a department should adopt my rule and that is "to resolve all doubts in favor of the department" and the citizens you serve. Lowering standards for police officers is not wise.

Police Training

Officers need to be trained in many areas besides how to use force and fire a weapon. Phycology, Criminology and Sociology are just two of the areas that need to be included. In New York, officers receive over six months training. The Academy is affiliated with John Jay College of Criminal Justice and many courses are taught by Professors from the college. A recruit will earn 64 college credits for successfully graduating from the Police Academy.

In-service training takes place on a regular basis to update officers on current events like new laws and Supreme Court requirements arising out of new court cases. Firearms training is required comes every few months to update weapons proficiency.

Using Controversial Shootings as a Training Tool

As a Lieutenant, along with my good friend Lieutenant Bobby Burke (Retired as a Borough Chief in the NYPD) and other officers produced one of the first "Shoot, Don't Shoot" training films ever produced in the nation.

The recent controversial officer involved shootings that have made the national news present us with an opportunity to analyze these shootings and use them to prevent future tragedies.

Just as we did in the NYPD, we can duplicate these events in a new training film designed to illustrate what the officers could have done to possibly prevent these deaths. It is a unique training opportunity. I would be honored to help this effort in any way possible. The training film could then be distributed to every Police Department in the country.

Mental Health Training

Research reveals that many people with mental health problems either keep getting arrested or even shot by the police. It is imperative that we get help for these people. Some are homeless after getting kicked out of their homes by families unable to cope with the behavior. As a group they are constantly being picked up in the street by the police and if the jurisdiction does not have and other choice they are arrested and held in jail for court processing. The cost to the Criminal Justice system is very costly as they keep on offending. Some cities, such as New York do a good job helping these people. For example, down in the Bowery which has always had more homeless people than any other part of the city, social workers are assigned with police officers to find housing and mental health resources for the homeless.

A "Hot" Proposal: Getting Rid of Rogue Officers

It is almost impossible to know before they get on the "job" that an officer is Racist, corrupt or will use excessive force. Once you become an officer, the "Job" changes you. Men and women who join the force are subject to the most intense pressure and temptations they will ever encounter. Some will become very cynical and some will become corrupt or brutal. A few can taint the many, and rogue officers can cast a lasting shadow on a department or the entire law enforcement community.

The best way to get rid of Racist and brutal officers is to monitor officers carefully "on the job". Who knows these officers better than the people who work with them on a daily basis?

When I was a Lieutenant, I created a whole new unit called "The Internal Communications Section" that worked out of the Police Academy. I created that section at the request of Police Commissioner, Patrick Murphy. He was appointed by Mayor John Lindsay who was quite liberal but generally let the officers do their job. The commissioner's office found out that I was creative and he needed someone to invent new channels of communication between the top and bottom of the organization. There was a problem between the largely conservative officers and a somewhat liberal commissioner that wanted to initiate some well needed reforms.

I was happy to leave the highest Crime area in Brooklyn at the 73red Precinct in Brownsville for a cushy day time job at the Academy. Raising five kids is a lot easier if you can spend some quality time at home.

At my newly created command, I created new channels of communication, such as a letter I wrote for the Commissioner, that I called "Open Door" in which the boss would relate some good new ideas to the "troops" in hopes of having their support for their implementation which is vital to the success of any department. In addition, I created a television Training program called "The Police Commissioner" which went out over the Channel 31 (the NYC channel). I wrote a short speech for the boss and then the commissioner would sit down with about 7 or 8 officers that were selected by their fellow officers to represent their respective precincts. It was spontaneous and sometimes contentious; the officers might relay some gripe that they had with a current policy or the disciplinary process. It was highly successful and written up in the NY Times. Commissioner Murphy was a great communicator and we got along very well.

We had quite a public audience for the TV program, even though it was primarily designed for training and, all officers would have to watch the program during in-service programs.

The reader might be asking, "What has all this got to do with preventing Police Shootings or Police Brutality"?

Even though I was in-charge of seven different units at the Police Academy, I wanted to create a unit whereby all officers would be able to express their concerns about anything at the precinct level either anonymously or otherwise. These concerns might be about Racism, Brutality, or corrupt activities taking place in their commands.

The unit was going to be called "The Hotline", officers would call to report any and all activities or actions that caused them concern. I was creating this unit in response to the problems officer Frank Serpico had when he was forced to go to the New York Times to report corrupt activities going on at a the vice squad in Brooklyn.

This resulted in the famous Knapp Commission Investigation of Police Corruption in the city of New York.

https://en.wikipedia.org/wiki/Knapp Commission

I wanted to create this unit to give officers a way to communicate corruption, brutality, racism without having to go to the newspapers to solve department problems. We could then become aware of problem officer's at the earliest time so we could get these officers dismissed before they could damage the department any further.

Ironically, many higher ranking officers did not like the idea of officers snitching on other officers through the "Hotline". They would have to deal with these officer complaints.

I was in the process of selecting officers to man the hotline 24 hours a day, 7 days a week. I had found some great officers for the job but needed a few more before the idea could be implemented.

All of them needed to be able to communicate an officer's complaint in writing to the proper division for investigation and appropriate action.

I was very happy that some African American officers applied and were going to be selected for the detail. One particular African American officer applied for one of the openings. As I did with every applicant, I asked the officer to sit down and write a paragraph or two about any topic he wanted to write about. The job required good communicators to relay the facts to the appropriate command whether it is the Civilian Complaint Review Board, the Internal Affairs Division, the Police Commissioner's office or any other office. The Black officer stood up and complained that he should not have to be tested since he had already passed the written exam to get into the Department. He then walked out of the room and the interview. The problem with his complaint was that the written exam is all multiple choice and does not indicate whether the candidate can write or not. In fact, a few officers luckily pass the entrance exam and turn out to be functionally illiterate. Their shortcomings show up when they have to write their first arrest or incident report. They then are dismissed from the force for obvious reasons. Officers have to write reports all the time.

The Black officer made a complaint to the Guardians Association which was an organization of African American officers. I was called to the Police Academy Director's office who was my direct boss. I found several high ranking officers at the meeting complaining about my requiring an officer to write something to make sure he met the requirements of the job on the "Hotline". I explained myself adequately but to my great dismay, the idea of the "hotline" was immediately dropped.

I think some ranking officers were looking for an excuse to scrap the idea since they did not want to deal with officers who made complaints that they would have to investigate or that might reflect on deficiencies at their commands.

It was ironic that an African American officer caused the collapse of an idea which would probably have helped minority officers the most. Shortly thereafter, I was transferred to a "High Crime" area of the South Bronx.

I could have caused a fuss by telling my friend, Commissioner Patrick Kennedy, the Police Commissioner at the time about the incident but I knew that some of the ranking officers at the meeting would become my enemies. I was already of the Captain's list and I did not want any problems to follow my future career with the force. The commissioner might leave when his tenure was up and I would be left out "up the creek" without a paddle.

About a year later, I was given the most prestigious award an officer could receive. In a very competitive process, I received a year off to attend graduate school at the State University of New York at Albany to obtain my Master's Degree and start on my Doctorate.

The very best way to find "Rogue" officers is to create a system that give officers a communication channel for their desires to get rid of problem officers. The idea was killed by several high ranking officers who did not want to deal with problem officers unless they were forced to do so by events involving the Use-of-Force or officer involved shootings. I loved and still love the New York City Police Department but this was a terrible mistake.

Chapter 6

The Constitution and the Use of Force – A Short Summary

In all takes place in an instant, the officer makes a life and death decision that is debated by the courts for months to determine if he or she was right or wrong. If the lower courts can not arrive at an acceptable decision between the prosecution and defense, the case may end up in the Supreme Court of the United States which may issue a decision that forms the basis for police guidelines in the use of force.

The Constitution is an amazing document. It is written in very general language so that the Court Interpretation may vary depending on the moral and legal standards of the times. For example, what is meant by the word "Unreasonable" in the Fourth Amendment on Search and Seizure? The Interpretation has changed over the past two hundred years based on hundreds of police cases brought to the court. However, the wording of the Constitution remains the same.

The answer to the meaning of the words "Necessary Force" in a State's Penal Code is very similar. Right now, we say that the police can only use force to the extent it is necessary to carry out a lawful purpose. First, the officer decides what is necessary in a particular incident, and then the courts try to fit the specific circumstances of a case into the current precedents of the Supreme Court. They don't often fit exactly and new instructions are delivered by the court that will guide the police in the future. If the officer wants to stay out of trouble, he must become somewhat of a legal scholar. He must make the law his own to protect himself from harm or prison. A decision made in the blink of an eye is often debated for months or years. Recent controversial shootings or use of force incidents have resulted in officers being fired or arrested for murder or manslaughter. In all too many, officers are killed because they hesitate to use force where it is absolutely necessary to save their own lives.

I had officers under one or more of my commands that died or were grievously injured due to the fear of making the wrong decision and ending up in the national news. One officer was faced with a knife wielding male that had assaulted someone in the street. The incident happened the day after another police officer was indicted by a Grand Jury for manslaughter for shooting a fleeing felon with a gun in Brooklyn. The officer in the former case kept telling the perp to drop the knife. The suspect was allowed to get to close and slashed the officer's face. He finally did shoot the assailant but, not until after, he was a bloody mess and required 60 stitches to close the gaping wounds on his face. He had scars for the rest of his live. He was only on the force for about 6 months.

The officer in the Brooklyn case was chasing a Robbery suspect who had fired at the officer as he ran around the corner of a building in an empty lot. The officer eventually fired as he thought the suspect would have gotten away otherwise. The officer could not find the weapon which had been discarded by the perpetrator somewhere along the route. It was one of those controversial cases with a white officer and a black suspect in a minority neighborhood. The officer was indicted as a result. It later turned out, I believe, that after the officer was convicted, it was determined that a teenager had picked up the gun and ran off. This information is related based on my own recollection of the incident that was widely reported in the New York papers at the time for which I do not have a footnote.

Use of force incidents often become the triggering excuse for violence by unlawful mobs.

The use of "Stop and Frisk" is another area where the Supreme Court defines what it means by Case Law and Precedent set by many cases that have gone before the court on the issue and instructs police departments about what the officer must show in court to legally defend his use of this police tactic. An officer must be able to articulate that he had "Reasonable Suspicion" to stop a person in a public place who may have committed, or is committing or is about to commit a crime. If during the inquiry the officer feels that his life may be in danger, he may "Frisk" the suspect by patting the outer clothing. If the officer feels an object that might be a weapon, he can retrieve the object and hold it unit he is assured that it is not a weapon or if it is a weapon that the suspect has a legal right to possess the weapon. In some cases the officer will then release the person when he is satisfied that a crime has not been committed. In many other cases, the inquiry may lead to an arrest.

In crime ridden neighborhoods, these "stops" often result in guns being taken off the streets. Aggressive police tactics take many weapons off the street and definitely lower the crime rate. In cities where the police are restrained from using these tactics, the crime and homicide rates increase.

In those cities where politicians are under pressure from the African American community to restrict police actions because of recent shooting incidents, the homicide and crime rates go up. At this time, cities like Chicago, Baltimore, New Orleans, Ferguson, Missouri and other cities are experiencing record Homicide rates.

The Use of Force Continuum

Almost all Police Department train officers in what is known as the "Use of Force Continuum". It is similar to a step ladder that starts with the mere presence of a police officer or verbal commands to a suspect and gradually, moves up to more aggressive or physical actions by the officer to obtain compliance with the legal instructions of the officer. The suspect's actions dictate what the officer's response will be up to and including the Deadly Use of Force.

The following diagram drawn by my Granddaughter Holly illustrates the escalating use of force which can start at any point depending on the actions of the suspect.

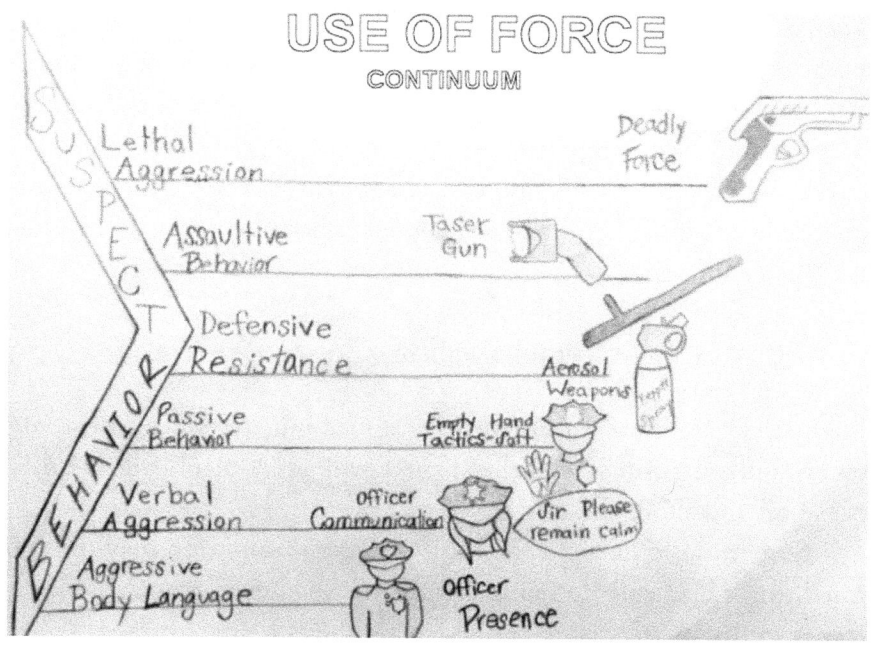

*Courtesy of Holly Agnew, Granddaughter of the author.

The Use of less than Lethal Force

The use of weapons such as nightsticks and Tasers have no doubt saved many lives but they are not without problems that the public may not be aware of according to research; it may be shocking to know that:

"Police have killed more than 1,000 people with Tasers since 2000".

Some of these "victims" had medical or mental problems. Some were under the influence of stimulating drugs which were already having effects on their health and hearts at the time of the incident.

https://www.pbs.org/newshour/show/police-killed-1000-people-tasers-since-2000

The reliance on Tasers by an officer may also be a fatal mistake for officers as shown in the following video where an officer tries to compel a robbery suspect to stop by threatening the perpetrator with being Tased. The officer keeps telling the suspect to "stop and take your hands out of your pocket" but the person ignores the officer. The suspect then takes his hand out of his pocket holding a gun and shoots the officer four times.

https://www.youtube.com/watch?v=884W4l3eoQg

Nightsticks are great intermediate weapons but the officer must win every confrontation or else the suspect will get control over the officer's gun and shoot the officer.

Sometimes officers in the heat of the confrontation may use too much force and end up being arrested or sued even if the suspect is found guilty of the crime for which he/she is being stopped. Police brutality often results in a guilty suspect not only going free but making a claim against the city and the officer. The Rodney King incident is just one example. Mr. King won a settlement of 3.8 million dollars and two officers went to Federal prison. As you may remember, he engaged the officers in a high speed chase, while drunk, exceeding 80 miles per hour through the city of Los Angeles endangering not only the officers but everyone out on the roads that night.

The police need more effective and efficient weapons to avoid fatalities in the future. The weapons have to be instantly effective in order to safeguard the officer and the suspect. As we have shown, that is not presently the case. Officers get sued arrested or killed by making the wrong choice on which weapon to use. It is becoming a much more difficult job with very little support from the public.

The psychological impact on an officer's attitude towards his job is changed when the community fails to support the Police Department. The "job" is hard enough without the added pressure that comes from community leaders in African American communities in the aftermath of a police shooting. The media fans the flames of increased animosity toward the police to the point that officer's pull back on what they normally do to protect the community. The thugs and gangsters take over the streets and crime flourishes.

One cannot force officers to confront suspicious criminal activity or deal with thugs, dope dealers and the like. Officers can become those that "hear no evil, see no evil" and do nothing. Cops can put in their 20 years of so without putting themselves in much jeopardy and happily retire.

The actions of a few errant officers should not taint whole departments and officers need continued community support to function effectively.

The media should be more responsible by condemning the violent protesters, instead of the entire law enforcement community for the actions of one or two officers in a particular incident. The community needs to be patient as investigations of Police incidents take time.

Police Departments in general want to be rid of officers that engage in brutality and corruption. Their Internal Affairs Divisions, Community Complaint Boards and local prosecutors can handle these investigations very well but, again, it takes time to sort out the truth in many instances. I remember one year while I was a Captain with the NYPD, 106 officers were arrested by the IAD or other elements of the Department without any outside pressure. The NYPD does a good job of cleaning its own house.

Chapter 7

"Stop and Frisk": Taking guns off the street and reducing the Homicide Rate

The False Narrative of one misinformed judge in New York City is that minorities are stopped more often than whites; therefore, the "Stop and Frisk" policy has a disproportion and adverse effect on minorities. Statistics may indicate that minorities are stopped more often but there is more of an adverse effect on minorities if the police abandon the policy. If the policy is abandoned or reduced, the impact on minority citizens will be far more adverse because of the increase in homicides and assaults with weapons on minority citizens.

Statistics are skewed because police manpower is distributed according to need, crime statistics and the density of the population. There may be twice as many or four times as many police officers in minority communities for several reasons. Some of the factors include population density, Crime Statistics and the sheer number of "Calls for service" in an area. In poor areas of any city, the police receive far more calls from citizens needing assistance of some kind than in more affluent areas.

If you have four times more police officers in an area, and all police officers stop the same number of people no matter where they are assigned. They will stop four times as many citizens in a minority area than any other area. This is not because of racism on the part of the police; it is because of the number of officers assigned and the amount of crime in the area. It is also true that in high crime areas the officers are much more likely to encounter people under suspicious circumstances. This also has nothing to do with racism unless you equate crime with a particular race or ethnicity.

Racial Profiling

City Police departments are often accused of "Racial Profiling" In my opinion, this is often a deceptive accusation by leaders of the African American community and the media. It is a popular refrain by African American politicians looking to boost their power and popularity in the community to blame the police for almost everything. The accusations are partially based on a federal report showing that about 85% of the people stopped and frisked were either Blacks or Hispanics (*Federal inquiry finds Racial Profiling in Street Searches, New York Times, 5 October 2000, pg. 1*).

The sad truth of the matter, according to research done by then Mayor Giuliani's office, is that in places like New York City, it has been found that about 89% of the criminal suspects were identified by victims as being either Black or Hispanic. Do these statistics mean that the police are racist or does this reflect the reality of who is committing crime in the inner city?

The "Crime Rate", particularly the Homicide rate has increase or perhaps doubled in some cities for a variety of reasons which are discussed though out his book. If the community does not support the police and insists on restricting what they can do, the crime rate will go up.

Liberals cite New York City and say that the rate has not gone up since the liberal mayor and a local Federal Judge have restricted the use of "Stop and Frisk". The impact of restricting this police tactic may take some time to impact street criminals but be assured that it will. It is easy to predict that if you put too many restrictions on a police force in the use of the best tactic they have, crime will go up.

The full benefit of "Stop and Frisk" is psychological in nature. If street thugs know that the police may stop and frisk them any time the officers become even slightly suspicious that they may have a weapon or if they may have committed or are about to commit a crime they will restrict their carrying and use of weapons. New York has some of the strictest laws in the country on the carrying of concealed weapons. If you get caught with a weapon there is a "Mandatory Minimum" sentence of at least one year in prison.

https://en.wikipedia.org/wiki/Sullivan_Act

When I was an officer in the city, the crime rate was very high. I remember at least one year in the 70' that 2300 homicides were committed within the city, most by hand guns. I did a study for a class that year in which I compared the homicide rate in New York City with the Homicide rate in all of the British Isles. There were a total of 198 homicides in Britain compared to over 2300 in the city of New York. The homicide rate is now about 600 per year because of aggressive police tactics including "Stop and Frisk". Without the "Stop and Frisk" tool and a growing lack of support for the police, I'm afraid the rate will go up rapidly.

https://nicic.gov/sourcebook-criminal-justice-statistics-0Footnotes

The majority of murders in the U.S. occur in only a small percentage of counties across the country.

The Crime Prevention Research Center (CPRC) said in a new report that there is a "geographical concentration" of murders, with 68 percent of killings occurring in just 5 percent of the nation's counties. The homicides also tend to be concentrated to relatively small pockets of those counties, the report said.

"It is stunning how concentrated murders are in the U.S.," John Lott, president of the CPRC said to Fox News. "And we show that even within these counties, with all these high rates, murders are very concentrated."

"These high [rate] counties have very large areas where there are no murders."

"In 2014, the U.S. murder rate was 4.4 per 100,000 people, according to the data of the report. If the deadliest 5 percent of the counties were removed, the U.S. murder rate would be 2.56 per 100,000 people, the report showed."

More than half of last year's murders occurred in only 2 percent of the nation's counties.

Looking at the historical data, the CPRC said that murders were even more geographically concentrated in decades past. On average, 73 percent of counties in any given year had zero murders from 1977 to 2000.

Take for example Los Angeles County, which had 526 murders in 2014 -- the most of any other county in the U.S. But parts of L.A. County, including Beverly Hills, Hawthorne and Van Nuys, had virtually no murders that year.

"Indianapolis, Indiana had 135 murders but only four occurred outside of the 465 highway loop that encircles the downtown area."

It makes sense to distribute police manpower to the 5% of counties in the United States where the majority of murders occur using "Stop and Frisk" and other tactics, we could reduce homicides and assaults in half.

Liberal politicians have always tried to restrict the power of the police or any of the agents in Criminal Justice system including prosecutors, parole and probation officers or correctional personnel. However, although some restrictions on the power of government agents are absolutely necessary, to diminish the power of the police to stop and question people in suspicious circumstances is a deadly decision and will cripple the police to the detriment of the community they serve.

Chapter 8

Policing the Inner City

I worked many years in the ghettos of New York City, starting my police career in the 32nd Precinct which was at that time, the highest crime area in the city. That distinction keeps changing as crime statistics dictate. I worked in many places at various ranks and assignments including Bedford Stuyvesant and Brownville in Brooklyn, little Italy, and the West Side of Manhattan. Out of uniform assignments included being the Lieutenant In-Charge of a Plain clothes Unit (Drugs and Vice Crimes) covering Little Italy (Home of the Mafia), China Town, The East and West Village, SoHo and Wall Street.

I was also In-Charge of the first experimental Street Crime unit and based in Bedford Stuyvesant and Brownsville in Brooklyn. This assignment put officers in civilian clothes or as victim decoys in bad areas and was so successful, it is now a tactic used by almost every city in the country. I was also commander of a Detective Unit and a Street Crimes Unit in the South Bronx.

I was also a Lieutenant in the Planning Division where I wrote along with my good friend Joe McNamara the disciplinary procedures for the entire NYPD. Joe, now deceased, was the former Chief of Police in two cities including San Jose and Kansas City. He became a consultant with the Hoover Institute.

At the Police Academy, I produced along with my friend Bobby Burke, the first "Shoot, Don't Shoot" training film in the Country. It was well named "Moment of Decision" and was bought by over 150 police Departments for firearms training.

I retired as a Captain out of the South Bronx. I know the inner city very well.

Every time you're promoted, you move to a new assignment. You also move as needs of the PD dictate. Sometimes, you can influence where you will work if you gain a good reputation with the "powers that be" In police parlance, "You Have a Rabbi" or develop special skills needed for various assignments. Inner politics also influences where you work.

The Inner City

There are mostly very good hard working people in the rough areas of New York. Most would rather live somewhere else but have no choice due to personal circumstance, a lack of a decent job or the lack of an adequate education. Many make it out despite all of these problems. God Bless them all.

When I worked in Harlem in the 50's and early 60's, people had great respect for the police. It changed dramatically in the late 60's with the rise of the Black Power movement, the Black Liberation Army, the Black Panthers and other racist groups. The Police suddenly became the enemy of the people. Police officers were being openly attacked and the shooters seem to take on a hero status to many young African Americans. Liberal minded Celebrities were raising money for BLA causes. Local political leaders praised their efforts. Several police officers were shot in the back in New York by BLA members. Two officers were killed on one of my old posts in Harlem. One was White and one was black, the following week another two officers were shot in the back down in the West village by the same group. This has only gotten worse over the years and the police are still under constant attack.

Making it out of the Ghetto

The people who make it out of the Ghetto are those who realize that their destiny is fully under their own control. They educate themselves, find and keep a good job and move themselves and family out of the inner city.

Many young people are trapped by a lack of motivation to stay in school. This may be caused by a lack of support at home, constant reminders by family members, some black leaders and others with the false mentality that they can't make it because they are Black.

Discrimination is alive and well in America, however, if you truly believe that you cannot make it because of your skin color, your own mind has doomed you to failure. Get past that notion or you will be trapped by resentment and anger the rest of your life.

A Black President and millions of successful people of color have proved over and over that the color of one's skin has very little to do with failure or success.

We all must die to the past and our prior conditioning and realize the present moment is the only time we have to achieve success. Don't let Color become a crutch to lean on. **It is a trap** just like the welfare system which is designed to keep people in poverty by well-meaning political leaders. The welfare system has become a way of life for generations of Americans of all colors. People who feel they have no control over their lives cannot succeed.

Blaming every failure on the nearest symbol of the political system which is the police is the mentality that creates the inner rage that is so destructive to the community.

A Prayer for the Inner City Child

God grant me the grace to know that I am the master of my life. I can hold no one else responsible for my success or failure.

Role Models

I thank God that I never had a role model and never needed one. I did admire some people when I was very young including my Brother Joe who was the leader of our local gang. I admired Joe DiMaggio and other sports figures but they were never what I would call Role Models.

Young students in my classes did not seem to understand the influence of Role models in the Ghetto. We all have differential opportunities depending on our own support system and the opportunities that are available. Affluent people say that all kids can find some job to do like delivering papers, mowing lawns, etc. Those kinds of jobs are not realistic for kids in the inner city.

Many inner city kids can plainly see that the successful people in their neighborhoods that have money, cars and girls are drug dealers, pimps and gang members. I asked my class what job they would take if they were offered the alternative of either delivering papers after school for $2.00 an hour or delivering drugs for the local dealer at $100 per hour. Which job would you take?

Very young children are often used by drug dealers to deliver drugs to buyers or act as lookouts to protect the dealer from arrest or search knowing that if the little kid is caught, the kid will not be punished by the Criminal Justice System. The child is kept in fear and knows that if he snitches, he might be killed.

I talked to one 14 year old drug dealer under arrest who was making so much money, he bought a new Cadillac. He was also proudly supporting his whole family. He was too young to get a license to drive so he hired a 19 year old to be his driver. Within the world of crime, he will go far as long as he survives his childhood.

As a result of multiple factors many young people find themselves out of school, out of a job and out of hope. They walk around with a mental rage at what they believe society and circumstances have done to them. It does not take much for them to explode. They may project their failure on society for not helping them. It is understandable from a psychological point of view that if you blame yourself, you will become depressed and self-destructive. It is far easier to lash out at society in general. Police officers in the inner city become targets as they are the only representatives of the Government that you see or interact with when things go wrong. They become the enemy.

Unlawful Acts by Police Officers – The Aftermath

When an individual officer commits an unlawful act by the excessive use of force or makes an error in judgement, the self -created inner rage of thousands of young people finds release in the anonymity of the mob violence that follows a police incident. The mob has no conscience of its own. Political leaders and the media refuse to take responsibility for any of the destruction heaped upon inner city business owners and innocent people who happen to be passing through the riot area.

For example, very few African Americans are aware that 54 people were killed in the riot triggered by the arrest of Rodney King.

Some completely innocent victims were pulled out of their vehicles by the rioters and beaten to death because of the color of their skin. One such attack was captured on video.

https://en.wikipedia.org/wiki/Attack_on_Reginald_Denny

Everyone is aware of the beating of Mr. Rodney King by two police officers. Very few are aware of the 54 homicides committed by the rioting mob. Why are most Americans unaware of these murders?

The media can distort the truth by glossing over some events and emphasizing others. The liberal media does it consciously or unconsciously and then refuses to take any responsibility for the mayhem that follows. This distortion of the news partially explains why most Americans are totally unaware of these facts.

The unlawful use of force against Mr. King was played over and over again. I think that I saw the beating video hundreds of time during and after the riot. I still see the video from time to time when the media wants to dramatize an act of police brutality by using the film as an example. The deaths of the 54 people were just mentioned like a passing footnote. If the media had concentrated more on the destruction and killings being perpetrated by the rioters, the riots would have ended sooner.

I was a Captain in the precinct where the "Police Tapes" were filmed. If you want to get a real view of what policing the inner city is like, view this documentary film which won an Emmy for best documentary of the year back in the 1970s.

I was assigned to the 44th Precinct as a Captain and was at many of the scenes in the film but my presence was left on the cutting room floor. The Howards were the filmmakers and they took a total of over 70 hours of film and boiled them down to a little over one hour. The officers in the documentary did a great job and provided examples of how difficult it can be to patrol the inner city.

https://en.wikipedia.org/wiki/The_Police_Tapes

In one incident, one young boy stabs another; both were members of different gangs. The boy lies in a pool of blood in the roadway between two parked cars when we arrived. The irate father arrives on the scene and is held back. We cannot tell the father or anyone else that the boy is dead as only a medically qualified person can pronounce a person DOA.

An ambulance was called immediately and hundreds of people attracted by flashing police lights pour out the old tenement buildings in minutes on this very hot summer night. The crowd becomes agitated when the ambulance does not arrive right away. Incidents like this turn into riots very fast. A few bricks and garbage cans come off the surrounding roofs into the street near the police cars. I send a couple of cops up to the roof and that stops.

Against policy and investigative protocol, after chalking the outline of the body, I ordered the officers to put the body in a patrol car and take the boy to the hospital. All the ambulances in the entire Borough of the Bronx were busy on other calls. This is not unusual. A riot is prevented. I order the officers at the scene to shut off their flashing lights before hundreds of other people are also attracted to the scene.

My detectives arrive and very quickly get the name and address of the perpetrator from the witnesses at the scene. The father knows the perp's family and they live right across the street from the homicide. The detectives stake out the perps apartment and arrest him when he comes home at about 3 AM. He has a very large tattoo of the Savage Skulls, one of the more violent gangs in the area, on his back. He is charged with Murder and convicted.

This was just one of the many incidents filmed in the "Police Tapes". I highly recommend that the reader obtain a copy or find it on Netflix.

https://www.google.com/search?q=the+police+tapes+1977+docume ntary&ie=utf-8&oe=utf-8&client=firefox-b-1

Chapter 9

Race, Politics and the Police

Politicians everywhere are responsible to their constituents... They also need to generate meaningful press to advance their careers. Police incidents are often a vehicle used to advance this agenda. National activists swarm to these unfortunate events like swarming termites to chew on the Police Department and the political parties of the jurisdiction involved enhancing their agenda for ambitious state or national political careers.

The larger the crowds, the greater the turmoil, the more publicity is generated in the local and national news. These events attract activists from all sides of the political spectrum. The media plays a large role and often adds fuel to the fire. As I mentioned in a previous chapter, the media is not just reporting the news but making the news as well.

In most of these shooting incidents, it is the situational factors that determine the action of both the officer and suspect involved. Race is not the determining factor on whether the officer shoots or not. The location of the event may be a factor in that more officers are assigned to high crime areas and are more likely to encounter an event that calls for the use of force. Time is a factor and the survival instincts of both parties cause actions to be taken on both sides of a gun. Fear of injury or death often determines the outcome of a confrontation involving the use of deadly force. Psychological, cultural and social factors along with the prior experience of the people involved also play a role.

Training plays a large role in all confrontational events. Reactions take place in milliseconds without the luxury of time to think. It is an automatic event propelled by prior training and conditioning.

Protests and other political actions will not affect future shooting events since most of them are situational in nature. If an officer hesitates to think things through, he will be dead before he can finish the decision making process.

As one example, I interviewed an officer who had an event with a knife welding subject. A day or two before this event an officer was indicted for shooting a suspect during a foot chase in Brooklyn. That officer said that the running suspect had a gun. No gun was found but the chase was long enough for the suspect to have discarded the gun during the chase. Someone in the area may have picked up the gun and ran off with it.

The officer in the present event said that he hesitated for fear of being arrested for shooting someone with a small knife. He let the subject get to close before he fired and was slashed in the face multiple times. He looked a mess and almost lost an eye. It took 60 stitches to close the wounds.

In a similar case, a Sergeant with the same last name as mine was killed by several stab wound in the chest down in the basement of a Bowery flophouse when he waited too long to fire. The perpetrator was also killed in that attack.

The police and the Criminal Justice System have always been lighting rods for both parties. One side opposed to police action in general except for extreme circumstances and one in favor of the police use of lawful force whenever it is deemed necessary by the a police officer.

Liberals in general do not seem to be attracted to jobs involving the use of force nor are they normally attracted to military service. Police departments and the military services by and large are considered conservative in nature.

Both liberals and conservatives are necessary in a democracy to avoid the extremes of ether. The national trend swings between both ideologies and when the nation goes too far to the right or to the left, the system adjusts. It is like the statistical bell shaped curve with a political lean toward the middle of the curve.

The Liberal Side of Politics

The liberal side or politics and the press do perform very useful functions by balancing out or tamping down the abuse of power by the government and the police. Examples of this are the establishment civilian review boards, advocating policy changes such as the wearing of cameras or demanding investigations when officers or departments show signs of dysfunction in supervision, policy, training or discipline.

Generally, in the Criminal Justice System, the left tries to diminish the power of prosecutors and the police to interfere in people's lives. They are against the abusive use of power of the law to compel anyone to do anything unless it can be clearly shown that the conduct to be curtailed is harmful. Curtailing the use of "Stop and Frisk" procedures is a good example. We discuss that subject extensively in Chapter 6.

The Conservative Side of Politics

Conservative politicians have the opposing point of view that we need more police officers and prosecutors. These officers also need more authority and power to safeguard the society. They are in favor of "Stop and Frisk" and other aggressive police tactics to lower the crime rate.

Both sides seem to be able to present statistical evidence to prove their opposing points of view. In the reality of the real world of policing, officers know that "Stop and Frisk" works to take guns and violent predators off the streets. In some of the more liberal cities of the nation, leaders in minority areas have convinced city leaders that these tactics are discriminatory against people of color in that minority citizens are more likely to be stopped and or arrested than white people. This is certainly true but many other factors other than discrimination can account for the differences. One probable explanation for the statistical differences is that many more officers are assigned to minority areas where the crime rates are the highest. If a high crime area has twice or three times the number of officers, this alone can account for the differences at which minority citizens are stopped or arrested. These areas are also home to most of the illegal drug activity of a given city.

The end result of curtailing the police use of these tools is a soaring homicide and crime rate. One only need to look at the increases in crime and violence in places like Chicago that has seen the homicide rate double in a very short time since the election of a liberal mayor.

Under great pressure from minority leaders, a Federal Judge has also ordered restrictions against the use of "Stop and Frisk" in New York City. We can expect, over time that the crime and homicide rates will increase in New York if the restrictions actually occur. Luckily for the rest of the country, the use of "Stop and Frisk" is still considered constitutional by the United States Supreme Court and that is not likely to change given the present conservative composition of the court.

Race

The police as a group feels isolated from the rest of society thus we have particular high crime areas with their own police created names and definitions. Names like Fort Apache or Fort Zindindorf in Brooklyn or Animal Habitat which was another name given to the high crime area of the South Bronx which was my last command post. I worked in most of these High crime areas. All of these names create the impression that the police are surrounded by a sea of hostiles bent on storming the fort. In this book, I may sometimes refer to the police as "the Blue Race" since they are often thought of as the thin blue line. Many TV programs also use this color to assign to the police. "Hill Street Blues" a very accurate portrayal of what policing was like in the South Bronx; "Blue Bloods"; "NYPD Blue" and a host of other TV show and movies designate the police as "Blue".

I think that many people would agree that the Blue Race is more abused that any other in our society. They receive more media scrutiny, are more supervised and misunderstood than any other segment of the society. What other workers in America are required to wear cameras and have everything they say or do recorded most of their working hours?

The Aftermath of Police Use of Force

We have all been witness to chaos and destruction that can follow a police action. A constitutional right to a peaceful protest often turns into mob violence. A mob mentality feeds on the media focus that follows. The media inadvertently fuels the fire of unrest by magnifying some facts and glossing over others to suit the political agenda on the left or right.

The best example of this was the Rodney King beating and arrest. Rodney King was pulled over and arrested for driving while intoxicated and leading the officers on a high speed chase of up to 80 Miles Per hour through the streets of Los Angeles, endangering everyone's life including the officers. Everyone remembers the brutality of the event since the video was played hundreds of times and it is still often played by the liberal media when it wants to amplify instances of police brutality. Two officers were tried and acquitted in State Court but convicted in Federal Court on civil rights charges and, in addition to losing their jobs, were sentenced to two years in Federal Prison. Mr. King was given 3.8 million dollars and served no time in jail for his role in the incident.

https://en.wikipedia.org/wiki/Rodney_King

It is simply amazing to me that when you ask people about the Rodney King incident, they remember the police brutality event but no one seems to know that 54 people were killed in the riots that followed. Many of these victims were pulled out of vehicles and beaten to death because of the color of their skin which was white. Only one of these events was captured by the media.

https://www.youtube.com/watch?v=u7Vte5e1luMSource
https://www.youtube.com/watch?v=z3V5UNUbM7k

In the Reginald Denny case, he was a completely innocent bystander. This video was far more atrocious than the beating of Rodney King but hardly anyone went to jail, thanks to the press seemingly ignoring the brutality of the rioters while amplifying the brutality of the officers.

Question: Why doesn't anyone seem to know or care about the 54 people who were murdered by the rioters?

The reader may not know about these victims because the media focused on the film of police brutality. They played it hundreds of times and completely downplayed or glossed over the horrific killings by African American mobs.

The rage of people in these communities is predictable when they have no hope for the future regardless of whether they were responsible in large part for their own failure. We need to prevent people from failing earlier in their lives so they won't turn into violent street criminals.

The best speech I have ever heard to describe the plight of the people in the inner city was given by my good friend and mentor Chief Anthony Bouza and can be heard at the end of the Police Tapes, previously mentioned. It is well worth the reader's time to listen to this impromptu description of the plight of the inner city.

https://www.youtube.com/watch?v=C_cfTHwBpJs

The Courts and the Police.

The Constitution and its interpretation by the courts govern what the police can and cannot do. The appointments of judges to the higher courts have a profound effect on police policies and training.

The court has been tilted to the right by the election of a conservative president in 2016 who has the power to appoint judges and this translates to giving the prosecutors and police more power.

At this present moment, the Senate has just decided to confirm the nomination of an assistant judge to sit on the highest court in the land. I have never seen the nation so divided as evidenced by the Senate hearings on the nomination of Brett Kavanaugh to the court. This appointment will swing the Court more to the right and provide the Police and Prosecutors with more power. The democrats were trying to block Judge Kavanaugh with all the power they could muster.

The Democrats were trying to block this nomination until after the Mid-term elections with the hope of gaining control of the senate. They could have then nominated a more liberal Justice that would have swung the court to the left with the hope of restricting the power of the police and the prosecutors. This was a monumental decision for the country and for the police as the Supreme Court controls what the police can and cannot do in performing the police function.

One of the latest police involved shooting case was decided on April 24th, 2017. This was the first case involving police shooting issues that went to the Supreme Court after the appointment of Associate Supreme Court Judge Sonia Sotomeyer. The case illustrates the idea that if the officer feels that his/her life might be endanger, he may use deadly force even though, it later turns out that the suspect did not have a weapon.

"Thompson testified he feared for his life when he saw Salazar-Limon reach toward his waistband, believing the suspect was going to pull out a weapon from under his untucked shirt, he fired a single shot, hitting the suspect in the right lower back.

Salazar-Limon sued Thompson and the city of Houston seeking damages for excessive use of force in violation of the U.S. Constitution's

Fourth Amendment. He is now a paraplegic and uses a wheelchair." (Excerpt from the case below)

"April 24 (Reuters) - The U.S. Supreme Court, turning down a chance to test the limits of police use of force, declined on Monday to revive an unarmed suspect's lawsuit accusing a Houston officer of unconstitutional excessive force for shooting him in the back after he reached for his own waistband.

The justices, over a dissent by liberal Justice Sonia Sotomayor, let stand a lower court's dismissal of a civil rights lawsuit brought by Ricardo Salazar-Limon, the drunken driving suspect who was left partially paralyzed after the 2010 traffic stop, against the officer who shot him, Chris Thompson."

The issue of police use of force has been in the spotlight in the United States following a series of shootings by officers of minorities in recent years as well as high-profile attacks on law enforcement officers.

"Sotomayor, writing in a dissent joined by fellow liberal Justice Ruth Bader Ginsburg, said the court's refusal to take up the case continues a "disturbing trend" of shielding police officers from lawsuits and rarely intervening when they act wrongly.

Thompson testified he feared for his life when he saw Salazar-Limon reach toward his waistband, believing the suspect was going to pull out a weapon from under his untucked shirt, and fired a single shot, hitting the suspect in the right lower back.

Salazar-Limon sued Thompson and the city of Houston seeking damages for excessive use of force in violation of the U.S. Constitution's Fourth Amendment. He is now a paraplegic and uses a wheelchair.

Sotomayor said the court should have intervened and reinstated the case, given that Salazar-Limon and Thompson contradict each other on what happened at the moment of the shooting.

'The question whether the officer used excessive force in shooting Salazar-Limon thus turns in large part on which man is telling the truth," Sotomayor wrote. "Our legal system entrusts this decision to a jury.'

Thompson stopped Salazar-Limon around midnight on the elevated overpass of a freeway for speeding and suspected drunken driving. While attempting to handcuff the suspect, the officer said Salazar-Limon tried to push him into traffic. Salazar-Limon said he merely tried to walk away.

While walking back to his truck, Salazar-Limon moved his hand toward his waistband and began to turn around, the officer said, prompting him to shoot. Salazar-Limon pleaded no contest to charges of speeding and driving while intoxicated, and was fined.

The New Orleans-based 5th U.S. Circuit Court of Appeals in June 2016 ruled that a trial judge properly dismissed the case because, given the perceived threat, Thompson was entitled to qualified immunity. Appealing to the Supreme Court, Salazar-Limon said he deserved a jury trial to decide whether Thompson was telling the truth.

In her dissent, Sotomayor noted that no gun was found on Salazar-Limon, and cited a 2014 decision by the San Francisco-based 9th U.S. Circuit Court of Appeals that said the fact that a suspect is unarmed is evidence that could discredit a police officer in the eyes of a jury.

'The most natural inference to be drawn from Salazar-Limon's testimony was that he neither turned nor reached for his waistband before he was shot - especially as no gun was ever recovered,' Sotomayor wrote.

Sotomayor noted that cases involving unarmed men allegedly reaching for empty waistbands are increasing, making it even more important that credibility disputes be decided by juries at trial.

In a separate opinion responding to Sotomayor, Justice Samuel Alito suggested that the case was handled both by the lower courts and the Supreme Court "in a neutral fashion."

(Reporting by Andrew Chung; Editing by Will Dunham)"

As in so many of these cases, the suspect is under the influence of alcohol or drugs. The officer and the suspect appear to be the only witnesses to the event and the court has to decide who is more likely to be telling the truth. We can see from the decision that the liberal justices on the court want a 12 person jury decide who is telling the truth and want to send the case back for a trial. The majority conservative justices find that on the basis of the facts presented to the court the officer's version is more credible. The office's version is given more weight because he decides whether he believes his life is in danger and not the suspect. It is often a matter of who to believe and, in this case, could a jury be a better venue to determine the truth? I think not.

From this single case, we can see how important these cases are to the future conduct of officers who must make decisions in a split second while the courts may take months to determine the outcome of the case.

Another example of cases that have made an important impact on police conduct was the case of Tennessee versus Garner (1968). In that case the judges took a more liberal approach and decided that officers cannot shoot a fleeing felon except under circumstances that would indicate that, if allowed to escape, the suspect would constitute a public danger. In other words, the case would have to involve violence or possession of a weapon by the suspect. For example, in crimes such as Burglary or Grand Larceny, the officer would not be allowed to use deadly force since these are considered property crimes and not crimes of violence. Three conservative judges dissented from the majority opinion and believed that officers should be able to use whatever force is necessary to arrest for any felony. It was a 6 to 3 opinion but had profound effects on the police use of deadly force. I personally believe that his was a good decision in that no one should be given the death sentence by a police officer for a mere property crime.

In one recent case, an officer was arrested for using deadly force when a suspect named Walter Scott ran from the officer most likely because he was wanted on a warrant for a misdemeanor when the officer stopped his car for a traffic violation (Broken Tail Light). There was a scuffle between the two during the chase when the officer tried to use his Taser gun to stop the suspect but since that did not work, he used his gun and shot the suspect five times in the back.

https://www.cnn.com/2017/12/07/us/michael-slager-sentencing/index.htmlsource

The officer was subsequently found guilty in a second trial in Federal Court after the first State Trial ended in a Hung Jury. The officer, Michael Slager was sentenced to 20 years in Federal Prison.

In a statement, Attorney General Jeff Sessions expressed his condolences to the Scott family and stressed the duty police officers have to uphold the law and protect citizens.

"Officers who violate anyone's rights also violate their oaths of honor, and they tarnish the names of the vast majority of officers, who do incredible work," he said. *"Those who enforce our laws must also bide by them – and this Department of Justice will hold accountable anyone who violates the civil rights of our fellow Americans."*

Under the Tennessee v. Garner case,

https://www.youtube.com/watch?v=5hhtkHm5VHs

The officer should not have shot the suspect. Often, officers believe that when a suspect runs, they must have committed a very serious offense. In many tragic cases that is simply not true. Offenders often engage in dangerous high speed chases simply because they are intoxicated and do not want to be arrested.

Liberal minded people want to limit the power of government and the police to interfere in our lives while conservatives want to provide the police and prosecutors with whatever power and authority they need to preserve public order and to protect lives and property.

Most Liberals do not want confrontation of any kind and I feel that they are not attracted to enforcement careers, such as the police and prosecutor or the military. Liberals are not likely to become officers but are more likely to become activists against the police for using too much force. There are always exceptions to this generalization.

Restrictions on gun ownership and the use of any force are often at the forefront of the liberal agenda. In order to maintain a semblance of political balance, the left side of the political spectrum is also needed by the country to restrain the police and prevent abuses of power.

Creating an atmosphere of violence

In our country, non-violent dissent and protest is a constitutional right of the people. However, well-meaning people often abuse these rights by unconsciously creating an atmosphere of such hate that riots and other illegal and destructive activity is either encouraged or ignored.

Ever since the election of 2016, the far left has refused to accept the election results. I have never seen, in my life time, more protests against an elected political candidate. The media is no longer just reporting the news, it is creating the news. Some in the media are grabbing hold of any story, verified or not, that might negatively affect the party in power.

Words have implications and can result in tragedy. The media widely reports any shooting or use of force incident that may have been unjustified on the part of any police officer. Out of 12 to 14 million citizen-police encounters, perhaps a dozen possibly unjustified incidents come to national attention. One of these was the use of force against Mr. Earl Garner in New York which is detailed in Chapter of this book. It was a tragic death on many levels and may have been prevented, in my opinion, if the officers had exercised a little more patience. A protest march down Broadway with some well-known African American leaders in attendance and up front as the protesters were chanting over and over again, "What do we want? Dead cops, When do we want it? Now"

The very next morning two innocent NYPD officers were shot while just sitting in their patrol car. One was of Asian descent and the other was Hispanic. There is no doubt that the criminal who did the shooting was encouraged and motivated by the protest marchers to murder these two officers. The liberal press should have but did not call for the arrest of those that motivated the shooter. They were just as guilty as the shooter.

The hateful energy that is now palpable in our country has created the atmosphere that impacts the police on a national level. Protests have become more violent. The assassinations of Political leaders, such as, the shooting of republicans that were practicing for the annual baseball game in Washington D.C. and the sending of pipe bombs to democratic leaders is taking political differences to the extreme. Recently, pipe bombs were mailed to President Obama, Hillary Clinton, and 13 other high profile democrats. Luckily no one was hurt.

If the next assassination attempt is on the President or his *family*, we will see more internally turmoil than this country has ever experienced. The media often tosses fuel on the fire to further fan the flames of hate. The protests of the Rodney King beating which led to the deaths of 54 people and police shooting event, like the one in Ferguson, Missouri after the Michael Brown shooting are just two examples. Words have consequences.

Celebrities such as Kathy Griffin, Johnny Depp, and other actors and sport celebrities seem to encourage, by innuendo, the idea of a possible Presidential assassination. Millionaire football players kneeling in protest against the Police and players like Colin Kaepernick wearing socks portraying the police as pigs, encourage hatred for law enforcement and the killing of more police officers by the criminal element in the inner cities who believe they will be heroes by assaulting officers. The killing of Police Officers by ambush is increasing more than ever as a result of this vortex of anger in the inner cities. Many mentally disturbed people think they are helping the cause of racist groups like "Black Lives Matter" who imply by their very name that police and white lives are not as important.

What protesters like the Black Lives Matter people should try to resolve is the question as to whether they are protesting the actions of all Law Enforcement or the actions of one officer against a suspect. If they are reasonable they will come to the conclusion that the objects of their outrage are individual humans rather than entire organizations.

Foreign enemies of the United States also see a great opportunity in a Presidential assassination to create chaos in the country to advance their own agendas. I'm sure they are working hard to see how they can assist in such an outcome.

In any case, the Police will still be in the middle; they will still ironically protect the marchers calling for violence against the police or the politicians who spread hatred for them in the inner city.

Chapter 10

It is not the color of your skin, your occupation or your Religion

We engage in compartmentalization thinking when it comes to groups of people like Muslims, Police Officers or African Americans. We assign them certain attributes often based on "reported" behaviors of individuals within the group by the media. Once we get to know an individual within the group on a personal basis, we shift our opinions based on their individual behavior and character; their color, religion, or occupation, is no longer used to identify them.

For example, once we got to know Barack Obama as an individual, the color of his skin no longer had any influence on thinking. His character, speech and individual attributes determined our opinion of the man. He was elected president with the support of millions of white Americans to destroy the notion that the majority of Americans were too prejudice to elect a Black person.

Americans seem to be overly obsessed with sex and the color of one's skin. In terms of sex, we constantly talk about the sex lives of celebrities, particularly politicians. Depending on our political leanings, we can understand and forgive the sexual proclivities of men like Kennedy or Clinton if we are democrats while condemning the same faults in republicans like Trump and Jefferson.

We tend to blame the color of one's skin as the cause of most racism which is much too simplistic to have validity. My best advice to people of any skin color if to accept what you have since you can't do anything about it anyway.

Science tells us that only about ten percent of our judgement about people is based on skin color initially and the rest, in my opinion, is based on the behavior of the skin you're in. It is perfectly natural to be comfortable with people that look like you and to be cautious of everyone else. This is true in all of nature. Crows do not hang out with Turkeys.

Go to any college campus or prison cafeteria and you will most likely see black students with other black students and Hispanics with Hispanics etc. This is perfectly normal behavior. Most of us would like to see more integration but it should always be voluntary. In some setting like prisons, segregation is the norm but it is not enforced by the authorities but by the inmate population. Self-segregation is enforced by racial and ethnic gangs with much violence against anyone who violates their unwritten codes.

Color is a big issue and the cause of much community unrest when a white officer shoots a black suspect even if the investigation determines that the officer was legally justified. One example was the infamous Michael Brown shooting by Officer George Wilson in Ferguson, Missouri. Although the officer was cleared by three different investigations, the first by a local Grand Jury, one by the State and one by the Department of Justice. The African American community has refused to accept these determinations mostly because the suspect was unarmed and the officer was white. The behavior of the suspect does not seem to matter and racism is almost always raised as the cause of the incident.

https://www.washingtonpost.com/politics/new-evidence-supports-officers-account-of-shooting-in-ferguson/2014/10/22/cf38c7b4-5964-11e4-bd61-346aee66ba29_story.html?utm_term=.98e5f608b7af

Prejudice against the Police

Perhaps one of the best examples of behavior of some members of a group being the primary reason for prejudice against the entire group is the resentment exhibited by liberals and many African-Americans against the police in general. Although the controversial shootings constitute a miniscule number of the total encounters the police have with minority groups, they are magnified beyond reason by the media resulting in distrust against the police in many communities.

One of the largest studies of the use of force by the police revealed that of the 12-14 million arrests made by the police in a given year, only .0419 percent involved the use of any force whatsoever. This included physical force like the force necessary to get the suspect under control or put handcuffs on the person.

Anthony Pate and Lorie Fridell, Police Use of Force: Official Reports, citizen complaints and legal consequences (Washington, DC: Police Foundation.

As of this date May, 2018, there have been a total of 337 people shot by the police. Only a handful of these have been controversial and made the national news. For example, let's say 10 questionable shootings a year make the national news. That's 10 out of 12-14 million arrest incidents. Even though the number is extremely small, the behavior of these very few officers in these events caused bias against all officers.

A FEW TAINT THE MANY!

68 officers have been killed in the line-of-duty so far this year. 23 of these shootings were officers killed in ambush without any preceding incident or cause; these officer were killed by pure hatred of the police engendered by criminal elements within the community supported by leaders catering to the worse elements of the Black community. One example is the March in protest to the tragic death of Earl Garner down Broadway in New York City with some well-known Black national leaders at the front of the crowd which was chanting, ..." What do we want, Dead Cops, when do we want it, Now!" The very next day, two innocent NYPD officers sitting in their patrol car were shot in the head. In my opinion, the leaders of that group should have been arrested for inciting the murder of these officers but no one was arrested. One of the black leaders at the front of the march was reported to be the "Reverend" Al Sharpton.

https://nypost.com/2014/12/21/there-is-blood-on-hands-of-those-who-demanded-dead-cops/

When an officer shoots an unarmed Black suspect, the suspicion is that he or she is racist because of the difference in skin color. The behavior of the suspect seems to be of secondary consideration by many in the community, if the officer and the suspect are of the same color under the same circumstance, community unrest is unlikely to happen. Color seems to be the deciding factor with the minority community regardless of the behavior.

African-Americans have reason to be defensive about color given the past few hundred years of being subject to rampant racism in America. That does not justify violence in the form of criminal behavior by large numbers of protesters after these events and even before a final determination is made by lawful authority as to whether the shooting was legal and justified under the circumstances of the individual case.

The violent protests that follow the incident do not target the individual officer but instead condemn the entire Police Department or law enforcement in general. It is as if the protestors believe that the entire Police Department must have a department policy of shooting African Americans. The truth of the matter is that each incident is determined by individual situational factors that have very little to do with color. If an officer is a racist, it could have a bearing on the officer's action just as the African American's behavior might be influenced by his attitude toward the police. However, by and large, the situational behavior of the officer and the suspect determine the outcome. Possible racist beliefs on the part of the officer do not pull the trigger, fear and the survival instinct does.

Protests against s particular department or Chief of police are justified when the chief has ignored past disciplinary procedures against officers who have exhibited racist or violent tendencies in the past. Departments must rid themselves of officers who have engaged in police brutality or who have verifiable racist tendencies. I had to order the arrest of more than one officer while I was with the NYPD. I remember more than one year where the department arrested more than 100 officers for various criminal offenses rang from Murder to larceny. The NYPD does a great job in getting rid of the bad apples but remember the NYPD has over 40,000 employees. Officers are not necessary saints.

As I remember my time on the NYPD, if an officer shoots anyone or even fires his gun, an investigation is launched. The Captain on duty submitted what was called "An Unusual Occurrence Report" which had to travel up the chain of command and be on the Police Commissioner's desk ASAP. The Captain could make recommendations such as forwarding the case to the District Attorney's office if a crime was involved; he could also determine that the shooting appeared to be justified or the officer could be referred for further firearms training. On top of that the shooting could be subject to a Grand Jury investigation. I have been to several of these types of hearings in my career. As some point in time, the department instituted a "Firearm's Review Board" which handled some of these incidents forwarded by the various commands involved. Things have probably changed considerably since I retired.

Each jurisdiction in the country has a different protocol when an officer fires his gun. Many departments are required to have an outside agency conduct the investigation so as to eliminate possible biases by the Police Department involved. This is absolutely necessary when the shooting is questionable or the community feels that the shooting was not justified.

Common Factors observed in controversial police shootings

Here are some of the more common factors from my research and reading:

1. An offense of some kind is believed to have been committed. It can be a major crime such as Robbery; it can be the pettiest offense or a suspected offense, such as the selling of loose cigarettes in the very tragic Eric Gardner case in New York City. It can even be a mistaken belief on the part of the officer that the

offender has committed an offense or possesses a gun when there was no weapon and/or no chargeable offense.

2. The suspect or victim resists arrest, acts in an irrational manner or disregards the verbal commands of the officer(s).

3. Drugs are found in the suspect/victim's body at the autopsy.

4. The officer is likely to be white and the suspect/victim is likely to be a minority citizen.

5. The community is dissatisfied with the police action or investigation.

6. The media magnifies the event with their very presence and often exacerbates and prolongs the unrest.

7. The politicians (community representatives) and activists of all kinds come from out of nowhere and everywhere to see if they can get some publicity for their causes. They tend to inflame the situation until it is out of control and the police call for state and federal assistance.

8. Damages are usually in the millions of dollars as businesses are destroyed and looted. Many of these businesses never reopen.

9. Many people are arrested, injured or killed by criminal elements in the community. 54 people were killed and hundreds injured in the Rodney King incident.

Conclusions: The few taint the many

Your color, occupation or religion is not the cause of things; it is the behavior of a group of people within the group that causes prejudice against a group of people that are of a certain color, occupation or religion. It does not take many individuals to taint the many. We certainly see that with the police.

When we get to know an individual within a group, "group think" no longer applies and we think and treat the person on his/her individual merits. For example, without the vote of white Americans, Barack Obama could never have become president of the United States. Many were able to put aside any racist feelings they may have had, whether conscious or unconscious, once they got to know the individual.

Chapter 11

Lessons Learned – How not to get shot by the Police

We have looked at many tragic cases of Police shootings, many of whom could have been prevented with some common sense instructions for those who might become suspects and for the police through training and better selection of officers.

Common Sense Instructions

1. **Don't pick up an object that might look like a gun including toy or real guns and aim them at a police officer, your will be shot DEAD, even if the officer was wrong, you will still be stone cold DEAD.**

   Research into many shootings indicated that many people are shot who aim objects at the police. You could even be shot, if you merely scare the officer by taking a shooting stance without a gun. It is possible that your family might be compensated in a wrongful death legal action **BUT, YOU WILL STILL BE DEAD**. Chances are also good, if the officer has a witness, a dash cam or fellow officer video, that your family will not collect a dime.

2. **Don't run from the police**. Running from an armed police officer, might cause the officer to believe that you have committed a serious felony such as a homicide or bank robbery, His/her adrenaline is already running at peak speed and a mistake can more easily be made whereby you can be shot in the back.

    The officer may not legally use deadly force to stop a fleeing felon, under the Tennessee vs. Garner case (471 U.S1, 105S. Ct.1695, 85 L.Wd.2s 889 1985). However, if he or she can prove that if allowed to escape, the suspect represents a public danger the officer can use deadly force. For example, the perp is running down the road with a loaded firearm and refuses to stop. There have been many cases along this line and the officers have usually been cleared of any wrongdoing.

    In the Walter Scott wrongful death case, the victim was only wanted on a misdemeanor warrant arrest and ran after his car was stopped for a broken tail light. Mr. Scott ended up being shot five times in the back during the chase. Chances are he would have been released on probation or minor bail if he did not run. The officer Michael Slager was arrested and was eventually sentenced to 20 years in Federal Prison. The Justice Department intervened and charged the officer with a Federal Crime under the civil rights act.

    His first trial in State Court ended in a mistrial when one juror declared, he could not and would not find the officer guilty. The vote to convict was 11 to one. He was convicted in the second trial.

https://www.cnn.com/2016/12/05/us/michael-slager-murder-trial-walter-scott-mistrial/index.html

3. **Don't resist arrest**. Many suspects are killed while resisting arrest. According to the courts, the officer is legally allowed to use whatever force is necessary to affect an arrest except under some specific conditions related to mere property crimes. However, often during a struggle, to arrest a suspect the officer may feel that his life of the life of another person may be in danger. The officer's perspective of fearing for his/her life is often the deciding factor in court cases where the officer is subsequently arrested.

Remember the officer's fear: if the officer is alone, he/she must always prevail in a physical confrontation. If the officer loses the fight, the suspect may then grab the officer's firearm and then, most likely shoot the officer. This has tragically happened many times.

The suspects may often die in these resisting arrest cases from either physical force, like the over use non-lethal weapons like Tasers, night sticks, rubber bullets and the like or choke holds which are barred by many police departments.

Sometimes, as was the tragic case of Earl Gardner discussed earlier. The suspect has a variety of health issues including breathing or heart issues which contributes to his/her death. The officers involved have no way of knowing a suspect's health issues until it is too late.

4. **Follow the officer's directions**. Many of the cases researched involve suspects who fail to heed the officer's verbal commands. "Drop your weapon"; "Get on the Ground"; "Freeze"; "Don't move"; "Get out of the Roadway"; Some may be more complicated such as "Put your hands on the top of your head and walk backwards toward me"; The more complex commands might be

difficult to follow if your intoxicated or under the influence of drugs, as is the case more often than not. If the officer says, "go ahead reach for your weapon and make my day", then you will know it must be "Dirty Harry" otherwise known as Clint Eastwood. Please don't make any officer's day and obey all lawful directions!

5. **Don't make any sudden moves**. Inform the officer what you are about to do and get his/her permission before you make a move. For example, if you're driving a car and pulled over for a traffic infraction or any reason, be civil to the officer, treat the officer with respect and you will more likely get respect back. Don't be upset, if the officer has his hand on this holstered gun. In many cases particularly if your kids are in the car and you apparently are not a danger to the officer, you will be let go with a mild warning.

    Remember, he has no idea who you or any of the passengers are in your vehicle. Don't mouth off to the officer. He will ask for your license and registration. Don't **suddenly** reach for the glove compartment or your back pocket without telling the officer what you are about to do. Let the officer tell you what he wants you to do. Be patient and move slowly and he/she will do the same. In a nighttime felony stop with other passengers in the car, the officer, will call for backup and when they arrive order everyone out of the car and to take other action to make sure the officers and all the passengers are made safe while the inquiry continues until either everyone is allowed to leave or a citation is issued or an arrest is made.

    Officers are often shot for being careless when they stop someone who has committed a minor traffic infraction. I had a friend in Harlem who stopped a vehicle for not having his lights on and when he carelessly approached the car, he was shot five times and killed.

In one infamous case in New York City, unarmed Amadou Diallo was killed by four police officers who shot at him 41 times in 1999.

The group of four off duty officers confronted the suspect, asked for his Identification and as he moved very quickly to his rear pocket he was shot a total of 19 times. The officers fired a total of 41 bullets at the innocent unarmed man. The officers were somehow acquitted but disciplined by the department. Needless to say, the community was up-in-arms about the shooting and rightly so. Three of the officers had to resign from the NYPD. The other officer fought to regain his job and was eventually successful.

http://www.nydailynews.com/new-york/unarmed-amadou-diallo-shot-killed-police-1999-article-1.2095255

In the more recent case of Philando Castile, the officer stopped a vehicle and shot the driver when he suddenly made a move to his waistband where the driver had a legally permitted right to carry a concealed weapon. The officer was yelling at the driver to stop moving and when his order was ignored, the driver was shot dead.

https://www.cnn.com/2016/11/16/us/officer-charged-philando-castile-killing/index.html

The video is very dramatic. The driver had a license to carry a concealed weapon and his girlfriend said he was merely reaching for his wallet that contained his license and registration. He, like so many others that have been shot, was found to have marihuana in his system.

6. **Don't engage in Criminal Activity.** This may seem like a simple step for most people but it is not that easy to do in the crime ridden inner city. The pressure on young people to become involved in criminal activity is very high.

    I give my student a lecture in which I ask them, if you were a poor youngster in a violent neighborhood and you had to choose between the following job offers, which one would you, take? The first offer, approve by a parent is to deliver papers before school and make perhaps $5 per hour. The second job offer is to play look-out for the local friendly drug dealer at $100.00 per hour. Which one would you take?

    A poor home structure with a missing parent means that your lone parent will be working two or three jobs to pay the rent and provide for the kids. You will spend a lot of time unsupervised and the temptation to join a gang or get involved in criminal activity will be greatest. The gang is likely to replace the family and the peer group exerts enormous pressure to conform to street gang rules.

    You're more likely to drop out of school to have a little money or to help with the family finances. You are less likely to have a good support system that will make sure you stay in school.

7. **Don't drop out of School no matter what!** If you have to drop out of school, get your GED and go back to school. I was paying half the rent at 12 years of age and all the rent at 15. I had to drop out of school and it took me until the age of 43 to get my B.A.. I became a Police Captain with the NYPD and a professor with two graduate degrees while raising five kids as a single parent. **Do Not allow yourself to fail.**

8. **The mentally ill are at greater risk. Unfortunately, we can't tell people not to be mentally ill, but we can still take steps to protect those with mental health problems.**

Often, the police are called when a person is acting erratically or is being violent. The responding officers have no idea that the person they confront is mentally ill unless someone informs them that this is the case. Officers need to be trained to deal with the mentally ill. These events may easily turn into tragedies.

9. **Don't be Poor and don't be Black.** I know we can't do anything about the color of our skin and getting out of the realm of poverty is not easy. If you in one or both of these categories then you have a greater probability of finding yourself at the wrong end of an officer's firearm simply because of the following factors.

You live in the crime ridden inner city.

More officers are assigned to high crime areas. More confrontations with the police are likely as a result.

The temptations of getting involved in drugs and alcohol are greater. As we have seen, the majority of suspects/victim have alcohol or drugs in their systems.

You're role models are likely to be those who have the most money who are likely to be drug dealers, pimps and gang bangers. They have the nice cars, the best cloths and gold jewelry. It is easy to get caught up in the world of what appears to be easy money.

www.ingramcontent.com/pod-product-compliance
Lightning Source LLC
Chambersburg PA
CBHW070129240526
45468CB00002BA/635